Public Planet Books

A series edited by Dilip Gaonkar, Jane Kramer,
Benjamin Lee, and Michael Warner

Public Planet Books is a series designed by writers in and
outside the academy—writers working on what could be
called narratives of public culture—to explore questions that
urgently concern us all. It is an attempt to open the scholarly
discourse on contemporary public culture, both local and
international, and to illuminate that discourse with the kinds
of narrative that will challenge sophisticated readers, make
them think, and especially make them question. It is, most
importantly, an experiment in strategies of discourse, com-
bining reportage and critical reflection on unfolding issues
and events—one, we hope, that will provide a running narrative of our societies at this particular fin de siècle.

Public Planet Books is part of the Public Works publica-
tion project of the Center for Transcultural Studies, which
also includes the journal *Public Culture* and the Public
Worlds book series.

Written

in

Stone

public planet books

Written in Stone

Public Monuments in Changing Societies

Sanford Levinson

DUKE UNIVERSITY PRESS *Durham and London 1998*

© 1998 Duke University Press

All rights reserved

Printed in the United States of

America on acid-free paper ∞

Typeset by Tseng Information

Systems in Bodoni Book

Library of Congress Cataloging-

in-Publication Data appear on

the last printed page of this book.

To my friends,

Akhil Reed Amar

Jack M. Balkin

Philip Bobbitt

Betty Sue Flowers

Randall Kennedy

Robert Post

Richard Rabinowitz

Fred Schauer

Acknowledgments

Perhaps the most unalloyed pleasure of publishing a book is the opportunity to acknowledge publicly those who have contributed to one's intellectual and personal growth. My primary acknowledgments go to the friends to whom I have dedicated this book. Each of these extraordinarily accomplished people has also displayed a wonderful capacity for friendship, reflected, among many other ways, in the willingness to join in countless conversations about the issues raised in this book. Although each person deserves at least a full paragraph, I will select only one for specific mention, for this book would not have gotten under way had Robert Post not organized, for the Getty Research Institute for the History of Art and the Humanities, an examination of contemporary problems of censorship. Indeed, parts of this book appeared first in two articles (now much revised) prepared for symposia linked with this project. "They Whisper: Reflections on Flags, Monuments, and State Holidays, and the Construction of Social Meaning in a Multicultural Society" was initially written for a conference at the University of California at Santa Cruz, in December 1994, on "The Constitution and Survivor Stories" and published in 70 *Chicago-Kent Law Review 1079* (1995). The panel at which it was presented included as its other members Akhil Reed Amar, one of the dedicatees, and a former student of his at the Yale Law School, James Forman, whose article on the flying of Confederate flags will be discussed at length below. I am grateful to Wendy Brown and Robert Meister for both inviting me to participate in that conference and allowing me to address the possibility that descendants of the Confederacy might be viewed as "survivors" with their own distinctive stories. (It was also a special pleasure to make the acquaintance at that conference of Wendy's and Judith Butler's newborn son, Isaac Daniel Butler-Brown.) A second paper, "The Tutelary State, 'Censorship,' 'Silencing,' and the 'Practices of Cultural Regulation,'" has recently appeared in Robert Post, ed., *Censorship and Silencing: Practices of Cultural Regulation* (1998). Excerpts from this essay appeared as "Silencing the Past: Public Monuments and the Tutelary State" in 16 *Report from the Institute for Philosophy & Public Policy* 6–11 (Summer/Fall 1996). Parts of the coda to this book also appeared in *Allocating Honor and Acting Honorably: Some Reflections Provoked by the Cardozo Conference on Slavery*, 17 *Cardozo Law Review* 1969 (1996).

Like all academics, I benefit greatly from the opportunity to present ideas to faculty colloquia. I am grateful for the colloquia at the law schools at the University of Minnesota, Loyola University in New Orleans, Western New England College, Boston College, the University of Chicago, Chicago-Kent, and the University of Utah. I also benefited from presentations to the legal history colloquium at Ohio State University, political theory colloquia at the universities of Vermont and Wisconsin, and a law and humanities seminar at Stanford University.

Many people provided invaluable help throughout the project. There are too many to mention individually (and I know as well that I would inevitably forget someone who deserves to be thanked), but I am happy to mention New Orleansians Jim Viator at Loyola and Judith Kelleher Schafer at Tulane, who were particularly helpful in providing information about the Liberty Monument, and John Paul Jones, of the University of Richmond School of Law, who fed me endless material about the debate over the Arthur Ashe monument in Richmond. Professor Jones was also kind enough to take the photographs of Monument Avenue that form an essential part of this book. (All other photos are mine.) I owe my knowledge of the history of the Millennium Monument in Budapest, which has become the opening subject of this book, to Kim Lane Scheppele, who sent me the fine chapter by András Gero about the monument. In addition, invaluable research assistance was provided by two students, Travis Vickery and Samy Khalil, and by Marlyn Robinson, a truly expert (and always helpful) navigator of the information highway, of the Tarlton Law Library at the University of Texas School of Law. Finally, I thank Rosa Eberly, at the University of Texas, who told me of Robert Lowell's wonderful poem, "For the Union Dead," which has become an indispensable part of this book. Indeed, until dissuaded by friends, I was prepared to title this book "Fishbones in the Throat," so powerful do I find Lowell's metaphor. Marc Galanter took me to the Madison, Wisconsin, city cemetery to see a special section set aside for the graves honoring Confederate soldiers who had died in Madison while prisoners of war. It wonderfully exemplifies the issues that are at the heart of this book.

I must also mention the editors at the Duke University Press, particularly Miriam Angress. This work was originally to be part of a collection of essays on multiculturalism. When it became a distinctly disproportionate part of that collection, Miriam enthusiastically responded to my scared suggestion that it be published independently. I was extremely delighted to be offered the chance to publish as part of the Public Planet series, especially as I admire greatly the work of Jane Kramer, who wrote the first book in the series, on public sculpture, and, more recently, has offered insightful reportage on the controversy over how Berlin should memorialize the Holocaust. Two readers for the Duke Press offered helpful suggestions that I hope they will see reflected in this final version.

As always, I remain grateful for the continued encouragement and support received from my colleagues at the

University of Texas School of Law. I must also thank the Boston University Law School, where, as a visitor during spring 1997, I wrote the first draft of this book. Finally, also as always, I am happy to acknowledge my continuing gratitude to my wife, Cynthia, and to my daughters, Meira and Rachel, for tolerating my various enthusiasms, which meant, on more than one occasion, being taken out of their way in order to look at yet another monument. Rachel deserves special thanks for trudging with me through the snow in the Boston Common to look at monuments.

Written

in

Stone

An Introduction

Their monument sticks like a fishbone
in the city's throat. — Robert Lowell,
"For the Union Dead"

Robert Lowell wrote these lines about the monument located at the northeast corner of the Boston Common directly across the street from the Massachusetts State House. It memorializes the Massachusetts Fifty-fourth Regiment, the first black regiment organized in a free state. It is usually called the "Shaw monument," after its central figure, Robert Gould Shaw, the white commander of the regiment, who was killed along with many of his comrades in the assault they led against Fort Wagner, South Carolina, in 1863. (Their story was the basis of the movie *Glory*.) Anyone familiar with the tangled history of race relations in Boston can well appreciate the power of Lowell's simile.

The monument to Colonel Robert Gould Shaw,
Boston Common.

Lowell could, however, just as easily be writing about many monuments in many cities and countries. Indeed, I will discuss public monuments in locales ranging from Moscow to Managua, Albania to Zimbabwe, not to mention a variety of American locales. In all of these places, one finds polities roiled in controversies attached to deciding who within a particular society should be counted as a hero worth honoring with the erection of a monument or the naming of a public space. Although as an American I am most interested in, and most of the pages below are devoted to, examples from the United States, I begin in Budapest, Hungary, with the fascinating tale of the Millennium Monument found there. Its vicissitudes wonderfully illustrate the central themes of this book; beginning in Budapest also underscores the ubiquity of the issues considered in this book.

The 1881 proposal of the monument, ostensibly to celebrate the millennium of Hungary's founding, was rooted —as is almost always the case with such campaigns by self-conscious politicians—in the political exigencies of the moment. As Hungarian historian András Gero aptly notes, it was also to function as a step in "an unprecedented drive towards modernization and the development of national consciousness—the main objectives of Budapest in its golden age."[1] To be sure, the monument that was actually erected in the first decade of the twentieth century included statues of Hungarian national heroes going back to the conquest that established Hungary and the reign of Christianity-establishing King Stephen, who in 1001 accepted his crown from the Pope. Moreover, the archangel Gabriel had his own freestanding statue in the middle of the monument (and rising high above the other two sections) to signify the importance of Christianity to Hungarian national identity. Yet, if Hungarian identity was depicted as beginning in the mists of the millennial past, it also was inscribed in a specific narrative with what its sponsors no doubt deemed a wonderfully happy ending: Hungarian membership in the Austro-Hungarian Empire under the rule of the distinctly non-Hungarian Emperor Franz Joseph. Had Bill Clinton been a nineteenth-century denizen of Budapest, one easily imagines him supporting

The Millennium Monument, Budapest, Hungary (1997).

the monument as a "bridge to the twentieth century" sym-
bolizing the marvelous promise of ever greater imperial
accomplishments. Thus Budapest citizens could observe
statues of various Habsburgs, including Franz Joseph himself, sharing space with angels and other national heroes
all incorporated into a satisfying story of national identity
and historical progress.

The Austro-Hungarian Empire (and Franz Joseph) did
not, of course, survive World War I. Indeed, when reading of the ambitious plans for the Millennium Monument,
it is difficult to avoid thinking of Robert Musil's merci-
less satire of 1913 Vienna, *A Man Without Qualities*, in
which hapless characters devote themselves to planning a
great celebration of Franz Joseph's extended reign. (His
reign had begun in 1848, the year of crushed rebellions

and other hopes for transformative change, which perhaps reinforced the illusion that the tides of history could in fact be controlled.) The power of Musil's great postwar novel in part derives from the reader's knowledge of how the story will actually turn out, a knowledge denied the happily complacent haute bourgeoisie and governmental officials who inhabit the book. Apropos the specific theme of monuments, one might well note Musil's own mordant observation that "the most important [quality of monuments] is somewhat contradictory: what strikes one most about monuments is that one doesn't notice them. There is nothing in the world as invisible as monuments." [2] Musil well captures the combination of hubris and pathos in the attempt by the monumentalizing generation to speak to and, ultimately, control the consciousness of their successors. All monuments are efforts, in their own way, to stop time. As Nietzsche put it, in his observations "On the Utility and Liability of History for Life," a "monumental" view of the past, a particular kind of consciousness instantiated in the physical stone of monuments, represents "a belief in the coherence and continuity of what is great in all ages, it is a protest against the change of generations and against transitoriness." [3] History, of course, moves relentlessly to mock any such beliefs.

The humiliating defeat of Franz Joseph's Dual Monarchy generated the emergence of an independent (albeit territorially reduced) Hungary. Nothing would ever be the same, including the Millennium Monument. In 1919 events took what Gero describes as "a radical turn . . . as the proletarian assumed power." Among other things, this led to a revisioning of the Habsburgs, who "were now presented as agents of feudal-capitalist oppression." Far from the statues becoming, as Musil suggests, "invisible," they were all too apparent, generating the same discomfort as a "fishbone in the throat." Of course, the thing to do when so afflicted is to remove the offender. The monument was thus stripped of its statues of members of the Habsburg dynasty, and the particular "statue of Franz Joseph — directly associated with the regime that had lost the war — was smashed to pieces." For better or worse, the radicals were rather quickly replaced by counterrevolutionaries who installed a monarchy whose legitimacy was based on the Dual Monarchy. Not surprisingly, "the Habsburgs resumed their place of honour" on the monument. Moreover, the site of the Millennium Monument also was designated as the proper place to put up a "heroes memorial." The specific heroes who were being commemorated were those thousands of Hungarians who had lost their lives fighting in World War I, altogether unsuccessfully, to "maintain the borders which had been in existence for 1,000 years. . . . Ironically, the memorial was thus dedicated to the soldiers of a war in which they had lost everything they had been fighting for." Like many other societies, the Hungarians proved themselves thoroughly capable of organizing their public psyche around a "lost cause." The site of the monument and memorial became "an inseparable part of the capital and a national land-mark," renamed Heroes Square in 1932.

Once more fate intervened in Hungary's destiny, as Hungary made yet another disastrously wrong choice in political and military allies. The aftermath of World War II swept away the conservative regime that had cast its lot with Nazi Germany; Hungary came within the Soviet Union's sphere of influence, and a Communist regime came to power. Once again the monument reflected new political realities, as the Habsburg statues and reliefs were taken down and assigned, almost literally, to what Trot-sky unforgettably dismissed as "the dustbin of history." In their place were statues of Istvan Bocskay, a seventeenth-century insurrectionist against the Habsburgs, together with reliefs of "his soldiers fighting imperial mercenaries." Substituting for the statue of Franz Joseph was one of Lajos Kossuth, the leader of the 1848–49 revolt against the Habsburgs.

Although Gero suggests that the Communists "would gladly have wiped the monument, with its archangel and kings, from the face of the earth," they did not do so. After all, they too could use it for their own ideological purposes of forging a new Hungarian consciousness, not to mention that they were unwilling to pay the potential political costs of destroying what had become a central public symbol of the Hungarian nation. Still, a "monument [that] was in-tended to condense the whole of Hungarian history into a single, complex symbol" with a unified narrative building toward Franz Joseph and his Dual Monarchy has instead, in "the different forms" it has taken, "faithfully mirrored all the historical and political changes which have taken place in the course of its lifetime."

One might well have mixed reactions to this tale of a far-away monument in a society about which most of us know little and with which few of us have any emotional identification. Is it a somber tragedy or a Central-European high comedy emphasizing the ironies (and roundelays) of history? No doubt it is both, though readers will undoubtedly differ on which aspects of its history merit tears or laughter.

The fate of the Millennium Monument and its heroes memorial is a perfect illustration of the central topic of this book, which is how those with political power within a given society organize public space to convey (and thus to teach the public) desired political lessons. Changes in political regime—sometimes awesome, as from Habsburg monarchy to Communist dictatorship and then from Communism to (some version of) liberal democracy—often bring with them changes in the organization of public space. States always promote privileged narratives of the national experience and thus attempt to form a particular kind of national consciousness, yet it is obvious that there is rarely a placid consensus from which the state may draw. In particular, organizers of the new regime must decide which, if any, of the heroes of the old regime deserve to continue occupying public space. And the new regime will always be concerned if these heroes might serve as potential symbols of resistance for adherents among the population who must, at least from the perspective of the newcomers, ultimately acquiesce to the new order.

As one might well expect, many of the best examples of these issues are presented in the aftermath of Communism in Europe. Some of the most enduring memories of my only visit, in 1989, to Moscow involve the public statuary, posters, and flags that dominated the urban landscape. My family found our hotel, for example, by reference to a giant statue of Lenin that hovered over the square where it was located. Many of the people I spoke to about the great changes then sweeping what was still called the Soviet Union found it almost impossible to envision that these statues would ever disappear. Such a possibility would have signified changes even more portentous than those already coursing through Gorbachev's Soviet Union. My last memory of the Soviet Union is the statue of Lenin in front of the Finland Station in what was then called Leningrad. Given that Lenin had made his fateful return to Russia in 1917 at that very station, that statue in that venue generated a special resonance and helped to constitute the psychic reality that was the Union of Soviet Socialist Republics. It should go without saying that it was truly unimaginable in 1989 that the flag displaying the hammer and sickle would have disappeared within three years.

No doubt the reality is far different today, whether in Moscow, Budapest, or many other cities of Eastern Europe.

Those who overthrow regimes often take as one of their first tasks the physical destruction of symbols—and the latent power possessed by these markers—of those whom they have displaced. Kenneth Branagh, in his film version of *Hamlet*, brilliantly evokes this by opening and closing his film with shots of what the screenplay describes as an "immense statue of a military hero," the murdered King Hamlet. At the film's beginning, it is as if Hamlet were still reigning, as is true in regard to the consciousness of his son, the Prince of Denmark. At the end of the film, however, the son (along with the murderous usurper) is dead, and soldiers of the Norwegian conqueror Fortinbras "tear at the great statue, hitting it continually with hammers, until with a mighty crash it falls." As the pieces of the statue fall (in slow motion), they "gradually obliterate the name HAMLET. For ever." Whatever the truth of the general proposition that "uneasy lies the head that wears the crown," this is almost certainly true of monumental crowns, especially when faced with an aroused populace who view them as symbols only of their oppressors. Perhaps it was the memory of the transformations of the Millennium Monument that helped contribute to what may be the most permanent Hungarian contribution to political semiotics—the toppling of a statue of Stalin during the ill-fated 1956 revolution.

Nor is Budapest the only Central European capital that could tell a vivid story about the fate of its statue of Stalin. As the *Rough Guide* to Prague points out, "Prague's most famous moment is one which no longer exists. The Stalin monument, the largest in the world, was once visible from almost every part of the city: a 30 metre high granite sculpture portraying a procession of Czechs and Russians being led to Communism by the Pied Piper figure of Stalin." The sculptor of this gigantic 14,200 ton megalith—which took some 600 workers a year-and-a-half to put up—"committed suicide shortly before it was unveiled, leaving all his money to a school for blind children, since they, at least, would not have to see his creation." Unveiled in 1955 on the Communist holiday of May 1st, the monument lasted only seven years until, under "pressure from Moscow" (then ruled by Nikita Khruschev, who had famously denounced Stalin and his excesses), it was "blown to smithereens by a series of explosions spread over a fortnight in 1962." "All that remains above ground is the statue's vast concrete platform," which apparently is "a favorite spot for skateboarders." *Sic transit gloria mundi.*

The *New York Times* thus rightly emphasized—by placement on page one—the moment in August 1991 when, in the aftermath of the aborted coup against the government of Mikhail Gorbachev, a crowd in Moscow toppled the statue of the founder of the Soviet secret police, Felix Dzerzhinsky. The statue had stood for many years in front of the Lubiyanka prison, itself the instantiation of the secret police and, therefore, of the worst excesses of Communist tyranny. Lawrence Wechsler wrote in the *New Yorker* that "monuments all over the country—fierce icons of the longtime socialist-realist hegemony—were being toppled and carted off" and, presumably, destroyed.

Surely, anyone who viewed this as a great moment for the cause of human freedom rejoiced as the symbols of the ideological walls came tumbling down? Well, not exactly. Even some strong anti-Communists confessed to a deep ambivalence at the destruction of these important cultural objects. Thus Wechsler quotes Vitaly Komar, described as "formerly among the ancien régime's most notorious dissident artists":

> This is a classic old Moscow technique: either worship or destroy. Bolsheviks topple czar monuments, Stalin erases old Bolsheviks, Khrushchev tears down Stalin, Brezhnev tears down Khrushchev, and now this. No difference. Each time it is history, the country's true past, which is conveniently being obliterated. And usually by the same people! In most cases, there weren't passionate crowds doing tearing down—it was cool hands of officials, by bureaucratic fiat. Same guys who used to order our shows bulldozed now arranging these bulldozings.

Perhaps it is thinkable that state officials should have used their power to prevent the destruction of these statues or, at the very least, not called in state-owned bulldozers to collaborate with the inflamed populace. It surely seems bizarre, though, to subject Muscovite political authorities to criticism for failing to offer a more vigorous defense of the earlier regime's tribute to Dzerzhinsky and to the secret police system that he was honored for creating. One wonders if Komar would subject Boris Yeltsin to similar censure for calling in June 1997 for a national referendum on removing Lenin's embalmed body from Red Square, where, seen by millions of people, it served as a central shrine of the Soviet Union. Yeltsin apparently advocates giving Lenin, some seventy-three years after his death, a decent "Christian burial." Needless to say, the Commu- nists who continue to dominate the Russian parliament are reported to be vehemently hostile to any such suggestions.

All of this is simply to ask, though, what one ought to think of the toppling of these and other monuments. Writing in April 1996 from Albania, *New York Times* reporter Philip Shenton notes that since the 1985 death of Enver Hoxha, "the brutal, eccentric, isolationist dictator of Albania for more than four decades," Albanians have done "their best to erase any memory of his crazed dictatorship. Statues of Mr. Hoxha were smashed and photographs burned. . . ." Ought the Albanians have been more respectful of the statues and photographs, at least as a way of acknowledging the past rather than trying to erase—or a Freudian might well say, with wonderful double entendre, to "repress"—it? Anyone taking this view would presumably admire post-Communist Berlin for maintaining at least some continuity with its past by leaving up on the Alexanderplatz not only statues of Marx and Engels, but also what a travel writer for the *Dallas Morning News* describes as "six stainless-steel obelisks engraved with photos from communist revolutions around the world." Interestingly enough, the paper captioned a photograph illustrating this story as follows: "Symbols of a failed system still have a place on the Alexanderplatz—for now." One does not know, of course, whether the "for now" reveals the newspaper's own ambivalence or that of the Berliners themselves. Especially curious is the *News'* description of a photograph of Erich Honecker, the former leader of what was then East Germany, as "all but scratched away by vandals." One might wonder if "vandals" is quite the *mot juste* to describe those who might resist the celebration of Honecker on one of Berlin's main public venues. Just as one person's "terrorist" is often another's "freedom fighter," so might one person's "vandal" be another's "cultural liberator."

As should be obvious, regimes in transition not only tear down monuments but build new ones. Thus a recent article about the Mayor of Moscow, Yuri Luzhkov, described by the *New York Times* as a Russian Robert Moses in terms of his impact on the Moscow landscape, refers to the "grandiose, $20 million, 150-foot nautical bronze statue of Peter the Great" that will, upon completion, tower over downtown Moscow, presumably serving at once to efface the former Communist reality and to establish a link with another period of Russian glory. (This overlooks that Peter founded St. Petersburg in part because he detested Moscow.) And May 1996 saw the installation, in the Moscow suburb of Taininskoye, of a monument of Czar Nicholas II, whose coronation had occurred a century earlier (and who was, along with his family, executed by the Communists in 1917). This monument, described by the Associated Press as "Moscow's only monument to Nicholas II," was destroyed on April 1, 1997, by a bomb. In condemning the bombing, Prime Minister Victor Chernomyrdin was quoted as saying that "Russia has already lived through the time when churches were blown up in order to assert the Communist vision of the world. Whatever our country went through—this is history. We, as Russian citizens, must treat it with respect." One wonders what "respect" counsels in the case of Lenin's tomb.

We must therefore come to terms with the transformation (or lack of same) of the public landscape of such cities as Budapest, Moscow, Tirana, and . . . And what? I use the ellipsis points not only to suggest that examples are legion, but also to refer to an issue linked with the destruction of physical monuments: the naming of public spaces. Consider, for example, whether the absence signified by the ellipses should be filled in with "Leningrad" or "St. Petersburg." And who, if anyone, is authorized to offer a definitive answer to this question? Some of us are old enough to remember Secretary of State Dean Rusk's insistence on using "Peiping" as the name of the Chinese capital, given that it was the then-unrecognized People's Republic of China that had changed the name to "Peking" (and, later, Beijing). Whatever one thinks of Rusk's specific politics, he can be interpreted as saying that one need not necessarily accept the attempts of victors to reorganize the consciousness of the onlooking world. In any event, "Leningrad," which survived a nine-hundred-day siege by the Nazis during World War II, did not survive the downfall of the Soviet Union; it has disappeared on contemporary maps, imaginatively restored to its pre-1917 rendering as St. Petersburg. (One wonders if Shostakovich's great *Leningrad* Symphony will be similarly renamed, or will Russian youngsters be taught that, as with the morning and the evening star, the apparently different cities of Leningrad and St. Petersburg in fact share a common referent?)

18

Perhaps we should view the change of name as a censurable act of state-sponsored cultural silencing, the extirpation of seventy-five years of Russian history, a submission to what is often pejoratively described as political correctness. Alternatively, we could instead describe it as the state's recognition of a moment of cultural liberation, the reclaiming of a different cultural heritage that itself had been ruthlessly silenced by those who wished to impose a Communist hegemony over Russian culture. The Communists, after all, had displayed no hesitation in changing St. Petersburg's name when they deemed it ideologically useful. (Indeed, St. Petersburg had, even before the revolution, been changed by the tsar to Petrograd in order to give it a more Russian feel.) And the decision to name it

Leningrad obviously takes on a wholly different valence from one to name it, say, Nevagrad, after the Neva River that flows through the city. It is hard to figure out why Communist mythmakers are entitled to a greater measure of respect, in regard to their politically motivated decisions concerning the naming of public places, than they showed to the mythmakers surrounding Peter the Great. Would anyone seriously protest, for example, the decision of a future non-Communist regime in Vietnam to change the name of what is now Ho Chi Minh City back to Saigon?

Names are important, and the ability to assign a definitive name is a significant power manifested, as significant power often is, in the most apparently banal of ways. As a sometime visitor to Budapest, I can testify to the frustrations that accompany using pre-1989 maps that still have the street names assigned by the Communists; most such streets have reverted to their pre-Communist names found now only on post-1989 (or pre-1945) maps. Street names are surely less dramatic than the names of the cities within which they are located, but no one ought to think that they are treated as matters of dispassionate routine. The kinds of passions linked to naming are well illustrated in contemporary Berlin, where local authorities have proposed renaming the Tempelhof Weg after Marlene Dietrich, described by the *New York Times* as "one of Berlin's most fabled daughters."[4] There is, however, opposition to this suggestion, and not only from local businesses who don't want the expense of having to buy new stationery. Other opposition comes from "older residents of the Schoneberg district [within which Tempelhof Weg is located]" who have "taken to grumbling that she was a 'non-German' and a 'traitor to the Fatherland' for her repudiation of Nazi Germany." She was no Elizabeth Schwartzkopf or Herbert Karajan, who remained, by all accounts, happily loyal to the Nazi regime; instead, during World War II, "she donned an American uniform as she sang to lift the spirits of Allied troops" preparing to take the war to her homeland. Interestingly enough, the street on which she was actually born is not available for renaming because it was earlier renamed for Julius Leber, a Social Democrat who in 1945 was executed because of his resistance to the Nazis. So Berlin cannot be accused of entirely ignoring resisters (though Alan Cowell, who wrote the *Times* article, notes that no street is named after Willy Brandt, who left Germany for Sweden during World War II, returned afterward and became mayor of Berlin and then Chancellor of the German Federal Republic). Dietrich is different. "She wore a foreign uniform and she never came back," according to a sixty-eight-year-old woman quoted by Cowell: "After 60 years abroad, she should be treated as someone who has betrayed the Fatherland." Perhaps Marlene Dietrich Strasse will become part of the Berlin topography, but that decision will clearly not represent a unified determination that she deserves any such commemoration.

The *Times* had earlier printed a story about Managua,

Nicaragua, and the difficulty of finding places there because many new streets, built in the aftermath of the disastrous 1972 earthquake, have not yet been named. This seemingly routine municipal matter was stymied because of great political difficulties:

At the moment, plans call for streets to be given numbers rather than names. In its 11 years in power, the Sandinista National Liberation Front named many streets for heroes of the left—including the one that runs in front of the United States Embassy here, which was called Salvador Allende Boulevard as a reminder to the "American imperialists" of their role in overthrowing Chile's elected Marxist President in 1973.

After the Sandinistas were voted out of office in 1990, most such streets, including Allende Boulevard, were stripped of their revolutionary designations. One main artery was given Pope John Paul II's name after his visit here last February, but the authorities appear eager to avoid political problems by limiting themselves to numbers.

"This is a society that is still much too polarized and divided to risk a controversy over something like this," a European diplomat said, "In this country, one person's hero is another person's villain, so something as simple as naming a street can become an eminently political act."

It is important to recognize that history offers us few examples of a clear and unequivocal displacement of one hegemonic regime by another. Historical reality is a far less tidy, and almost infinitely more messy, enterprise than that suggested by many national myths. After all, it is rarely the case that partisans of the displaced regime actually exit from the historical stage. Ironically enough, one of the tidiest examples of transformation was the American Revolution, where the losing loyalists had the good grace to accept exile (or return "home," as the case may be) in England or in Canada. Almost no active supporters of the discredited regime remained to speak of the merits of King George and his associates or to demand some public recognition of their contributions to the creation of what would become the United States. This certainly helps to explain why there is no full-scale monument to Benedict Arnold in the United States, even though his skills of generalship, revealed at the Battle of Saratoga prior to his defection to the English cause, contributed mightily to there being a United States at all. (This must be understood in the context of the fact that there apparently is a monument at the site of the battle, but it consists only of the feet of an unnamed general. The cognoscenti know that this is in fact a limited tribute to Arnold.)

Perhaps the most important question is what happens to public space when the political and cultural cleavages within a given society are fully manifested and even, as in some versions of multiculturalism, endorsed. Consider another example involving street-naming, from the United States. The February 15, 1997, *New York Times* included a story, "Another Proposal to Rename a Street Upsets San Franciscans," detailing the debate over a proposal, by Dr. Amos Brown, "the lone black member of the [San Francisco] Board of Supervisors" to rename Fillmore Street after "a local civil rights hero, Dr. Carlton B. Goodlett." Brown, noting that Fillmore Street commemorates President Millard Fillmore, one of whose most noteworthy deeds was signing the Fugitive Slave Act of 1850, said, "Here's a person who worked to keep our forebears in the cruel system of slavery." One can be confident, of course, that San Francisco's desire to honor our oft-ignored thirteenth President had far less to do with his views on slavery than with the fact that one of the other bills he signed, as part of the so-called Compromise of 1850 that staved off civil war for a decade, included California's admission to the Union (as a free state). And, whatever the origins of Fillmore Street, one can be confident that most contemporaries identify it as the location of Bill Graham's legendary rock venue, the Fillmore, one of the major sources of the counterculture of the 1960s. San Francisco's usually voluble mayor, Willie Brown, said only, "You have to be very careful with the street-naming process."

One doubts that many people care about the fate of memorials to Millard Fillmore. However, this is most certainly not the case with regard to George Washington, "the father of our country." Much public debate ensued, therefore, following the October 27, 1997, decision by the (New) Orleans Parish School Board, which had adopted a policy prohibiting naming schools after "former slave owners or others who did not respect equal opportunity for all," to change the name of the George Washington Elementary School, which will now be known as Dr. Charles Richard Drew Elementary School. Drew was an African American surgeon best known, according to the *New York Times*, "for developing methods to preserve blood plasma and for protesting the United States Army's practice of segregating donated blood by race."[5] Editorials, op-ed essays, and letters to the editor debated the propriety of the New Orleans policy in general and of its application to Washington in particular. I note that far less controversy was stirred, at least nationally, by the decision to remove from a junior high school the name of Confederate general P. G. T. Beauregard and to replace it with the name of Thurgood Marshall.

The point is that though one might well analyze San Francisco or New Orleans as ever-changing societies, one would still hesitate to use the language of "regime change" that comes more naturally to analysis of Eastern Europe. Instead, the changes involve more the entry of new groups into the ambit of those with genuine political clout, with the consequent necessity of responding to the demands of these groups. As the eminent sociologist Nathan Glazer writes in the revealingly titled *We Are All Multiculturalists Now*, multiculturalism "raises the general question of how we are to understand our nation and its culture. What monuments are we to raise (or raze), what holidays are we to celebrate, how are we to name our schools and our streets?" Ironically enough, the answer to these questions may be easier in localities that undergo sharply delineated regime changes than in countries wrestling with the prob- lems of achieving a truly multicultural identity. Do we, then, have political and legal theories adequate to assess the fate of the Millennium Monument or, far closer to home, to determine who is a suitable candidate for inclusion along Monument Avenue in Richmond, Virginia? If one, for example, offers the contemptuous epithet "Stalinist" to describe the suggestion (discussed at length below) that one destroy a monument to Louisiana racists who attempted to overthrow the biracial Reconstruction government, then why not condemn as "Stalinist" the removal, in Russia and other successor states within the former Communist empire, of statues of Stalin and Lenin from public squares and their replacement with what are thought to be more fitting figures of public honor?

One potential solution is to add new statues without displacing the old. So, for example, a statue of Andrey Sakharov or, for that matter, Aleksandr Solzhenitsyn, could share space with their persecutor Leonid Brezhnev, just as Imre Nagy and Janos Kadar have graves together in Budapest's Kerepesi Cemetary—and rallies commemorating both funerals were held at Heroes Square—though it was Kadar who had Nagy, a leader of the 1956 insurrection against the Soviet Union, executed as a traitor. (And, as a matter of fact, it is Nagy who is honored in a moving statue about a block from the Hungarian parliament.) Perhaps the ability to accept such a sharing represents political maturity and acknowledgment of the almost endless complexity of political life, though one might be excused for believing that political language takes on Orwellian aspects when we equally honor insurgents and executioners. In any event, we might be curious about which societies could agree to pay equal homage to ideological opposites and which, on the other hand, choose a more consistent group of honorees.

Although most of the examples up to now have been drawn from "foreign" locales, there is certainly no lack of similar controversies in the United States. It is a notorious truth that the United States is home to an ever-more-fractionated population tempted to engage in what has come to be termed "identity politics." And, of course, everyone (or at least everyone so disposed) can play the identity politics game. Indeed, once one becomes aware of the issue, it is almost literally impossible to pick up any issue of a newspaper or magazine without finding examples in our own times and settings. Let me offer four, before moving to the examples that will be the central focus of this book. First, a Connecticut town recently decided to move "an imposing statue of Capt. John Mason" because of protests by American Indians that, far from being a heroic English settler, he is in fact better described as one who had massacred the Pequot Indians in 1637. As the writer for *The Hartford Courant* noted, the discussion about the fate of the statue is part not only of "a wider historical debate over whether American history, much of it written decades ago by European descendants, accurately reflected the role of Native Americans," but also a reflection of "the reemergence of the Pequot tribe as a powerful regional influence" in the Connecticut of 1995.

The second example comes from the opposite coast. A *New York Times* article, "San Francisco Journal: Century-Old Monument Feels the Clash of History,"[6] tells of the discord provoked by the Pioneer Monument, a "huge granite pedestal topped by a bronze statue [that] has four life-sized groups of sculpture around the base, including one that shows an Indian on the ground, with a friar standing over him who is pointing to heaven and a Spanish vaquero raising a hand in triumph." The monument was moved from what had become a somewhat seedy area of the city to a place "between the old and new libraries and across a park from the new City Hall." However, "preservationists objected to moving the statue at all; Indians wanted it junked." Thus one member of the American Indian Movement Confederation described the monument as "symboliz[ing] the humiliation, degradation, genocide and sorrow inflicted upon this country's indigenous people by a foreign invader, through religious persecution and ethnic prejudice." The solution to such objections was a decision by the city's Art Commission to "install a brass plaque to explain the misfortunes suffered by the indigenous population." Lest one believe that this offered any easy way out, note that the original draft of the plaque— "With their efforts over in 1834, the missionaries left behind about 56,000 converts—and 150,000 dead. Half the original Native American population had perished during this time from disease, armed attacks and mistreatment."—provoked angry responses both from a Catholic Archbishop of the Archdiocese of San Francisco and the consul general of Spain. Moreover, Kevin Starr, the most distinguished contemporary historian of California's past, complained that the wording was "a horrible and hateful distortion of the truth," while yet other commentators suggested that it was in fact too easy on the church. Following extended debate the Art Commission voted to delete "and 150,000 dead" as well as to add a phrase that, in the words of the *New York Times* reporter, "attribut[es] the decline of the Indian population to European contact, taking the onus off the church. The commission also discussed soliciting an additional monument giving the Indian point of view." I note without additional comment the bland assumption that there is a single "Indian point of view."

Moving to our nation's capital, we find a wonderful contretemps surrounding the decision by Congress, after some seventy-five years, to place a statue of three female suffragists—Susan B. Anthony, Elizabeth Cady Stanton, and Lucretia Mott—in the rotunda of the Capitol. The statue had originally been donated to Congress by the National Women's Party in 1921, in part because all of the statues displayed at the Capitol were of men. It was, however, consigned to the crypt of the Capitol, in part, allegedly, because of aesthetic objections to the sculpture, which, according to the *Washington Post,* had been "deliberately left . . . in an unfinished state to signify that the struggle of women would continue with future generations." One might think that the final decision to place the work in the rotunda would receive general applause, but this is not the case. The National Political Congress of Black Women protests that the "statue does not represent the suffragette movement" in its entirety. According to C. Delores Tucker, chair of the congressional black women's congress, "It's wrong and we're going to do everything we can to stop it. We have been left out of history too much and we're not going to be left out anymore." The solution, according to the protesters, is to add to the statue a depiction of Sojourner Truth, the black nineteenth-century feminist-abolitionist. This was, incidentally, only one of the "monumental" controversies roiling Washington in the spring of 1997. There was also the fight over how FDR would be depicted—in a wheelchair or not, holding his signature cigarette holder or empty-handed—in his long-delayed monument, which finally opened in May 1997, as well as a struggle over the placement on the National Mall of a new monument to the veterans of World War II.

Finally, in a June 23, 1996, story aptly titled "Little Bighorn Again Inspires Passion," the *New York Times* details some of the plans that the new superintendent of the Little Bighorn Battlefield National Monument, Gerard Baker, a Mandan Hidatsa Indian, has for the site. Baker's desire is to make the site "more user friendly for Indians," which

involves, among other things, supplementing the present monument honoring the U.S. soldiers slain during what used to be known as Custer's Last Stand with a new monument that would commemorate the fifty Indians who died in the Battle of the Little Bighorn. And he would like to put that monument on Last Stand Hill, just yards from the monument to the U.S. soldiers. The *Times* quotes Bob Wells, an editor of the *Custer Little Bighorn Battlefield Advocate:* "Gerard has a crusade going, the Indianization of the battlefield. He's gone way overboard. It would be a serious mistake to plant the Indian Memorial anywhere near the memorial of the Seventh Cavalry. The magnetism and dignity of that monument is that it occupies that hill." To put it mildly, one would be surprised if there is any consensus on what counts as going "overboard" or whether the "Indianization" of the site of one of the few triumphs over the conquering United States Army is necessarily something to be criticized. One should note that Baker also endorsed an Indian celebration of the 120th anniversary of the battle that would include the Indians riding on horses to the gravesite where the two hundred U.S. soldiers are buried and "counting coup" by hitting with a stick the stone obelisk marking the grave. According to the *Times*, "Counting coup was a battle tradition in which warriors proved their skill and courage by striking an enemy with a special stick and returning safely to the tribe." As to this, Wells asks, "What would people say if cavalry re-enactors went to Wounded Knee and touched the monument [to the Sioux dead] with sabers?" Upon being asked whether Baker in effect was supporting the gloating by Indians of their victory at Little Bighorn, Baker said, "That's right. It's about time." I cannot resist noting the wonderful double entendre of this last phrase, for, of course, monuments are quintessentially "about time" and who shall control the meaning assigned to Proustian moments of past time.

All regions of the country no doubt offer fit examples for discussion. The rest of this book, however, focuses on the American South. One reason, perhaps, is that it is the region I most call home, having been born and raised in North Carolina and having lived now for eighteen years in Austin, Texas. Beyond this parochial reason, though, is the fact that the issues presented by the South, as a distinctive region of our nation, have, since the founding of our nation, presented the most exquisite difficulties in terms of establishing a truly coherent national identity. Although both were formally English, one can

hardly amalgamate the Puritan "Roundheads" who settled
New England with the "Cavaliers" who founded Virginia,
let alone the Scotch-Irish who dominated the settlements
in the lower South, and the cultural differences between
North and South have been a staple of those who would
analyze America at least since the nineteenth century.
Even if it took until recently to coin the term, "multiculturalism" has long been the reality in the United States.
My particular concern is the following: Do we, as a society,
have a duty to the past to continue to give pride of sacred
place to monuments to our — and what one means by "our"
is perhaps the central question of this essay — own "Lost
Cause" of the Confederate States of America in spite of
altogether persuasive arguments not only that this cause
was racist at its core, but also that some of the specific
monuments, such as New Orleans's Liberty Monument,
leave nothing to the imagination in terms of their racism?

These are scarcely academic questions, at least in the
pejorative sense of treating the academy as the place for
idle speculation about things that scarcely concern ordinary Americans. Within a recent week, for example, two
of our leading national newspapers published stories illustrating the depth of such issues within the contemporary
culture. "A Confederate Flag Vexes America Once Again,
As Southerners Battle Each Other Over Heritage," stated
the February 4, 1997, *Wall Street Journal* as it reported
on the controversy raging through South Carolina as to
whether the Confederate battle flag should be removed

from its present place of honor atop the South Carolina capitol, where it has flown since 1962. (More shall be said below about the importance of that date.) Although Governor David Beasley, who has proposed that the flag come down, is a Republican (as is, of course, Senator Strom Thurmond, who, along with three other Republican former governors, supported Beasley's proposal), the Republican-controlled House of Representatives refused to go along. It settled for submitting the issue to a referendum of South Carolina voters. Interestingly enough, even the so-called "Heritage Act" submitted by the governor would, according to the *Journal,* "protect the names of all streets, monuments and public squares bearing the names 'of our Confederate leaders.' "

The *New York Times* in turn placed on its front page a story, "Symbols of Old South Feed a New Bitterness."[7] Though it, too, referred to the South Carolina flag controversy, it noted as well the increasing acrimony over statues to the Confederate war dead. This being America, the *Times* notes that at least one lawsuit has been filed, in Franklin, Tennessee, seeking not only removal of a statue of a Confederate soldier that towers over the town square but also $44 million in damages. Charles Reagan Wilson, a University of Mississippi historian, is quoted as observing that such battles "really deal with issues of identity and world view and ethnicity. Are we one people or two?" To force white southerners to lower the flag or take down the monuments and, therefore, "to cut that tie with the symbols, with the genealogy, is for them a kind of cultural death." As if directly corroborating this analysis, the *Times* quotes a South Carolina legislator who describes his opponents as demanding nothing less than "cultural genocide."

It is worth noting how much this legislator and his allies are adopting the language of cultural victimization that one often expects to hear from sources other than Southern white males. In this regard consider some remarkable sentences from Eugene Genovese's recent book, *The Southern Tradition: The Achievement and Limitations of an American Conservatism.* Genovese, one of our leading analysts of American slavery and of Southern culture, who gained fame as an explicitly Marxist historian, confesses at the outset that part of his interest in the specifically conservative aspects of the Southern tradition comes from his dismay at the " 'modernization' that is transforming the South" in which he now lives. While recognizing the beneficial aspects of such changes, including "long overdue if incomplete justice for black people," he is also concerned with the "price" accompanying modernization, which, he says, "includes a neglect of, or contempt for, the history of southern whites, without which some of the more distinct and noble features of American national life must remain incomprehensible." "The northern victory in 1865 silenced a discretely southern interpretation of American history and national identity, and it promoted a contemptuous dismissal of all things southern as nasty, racist, immoral, and intellectually inferior." The language shortly escalates into the assertion that "we are witnessing" nothing less than "a cultural and political atrocity — an increasingly successful campaign by the media and an academic elite to strip young white southerners, and arguably black southerners as well, of their heritage, and therefore, their identity." In a brilliant rhetorical move, Genovese completes his preface by quoting from W. E. B. DuBois's essay on Atlanta, in which that most radical of all African American historians, who introduced all of us to the multiple consciousnesses contained within the deceptive term

"American," nonetheless reminded his readers "that with all the Bad that fell" with the defeat of the Old South, "something was vanquished that deserved to live. . . ."

Given a cultural atmosphere where many worry about the silencing of those who have been the victims of various political movements, it is especially worth noting Genovese's appropriation of the language of silencing and his lament for the concomitant negation of the political and cultural identities of some of our fellow Americans. He calls for the recognition of the dignity of those who have been silenced and who should, therefore, be allowed to speak their own tongue, however potentially grating the sound. Can one take such claims seriously in the context of those who speak on behalf of the white survivors of the great war of 1861–65 and of the culture formed in part to limit the consequences of the defeat at Appomattox? One wonders how Genovese would respond to recent efforts by University of Mississippi Chancellor Robert C. Khayat to

35

encourage what the *New York Times* has described as "a period of campus-wide self-analysis that could lead to the elimination" of the various Confederate symbols "that are regarded as sacred at this most tradition-bound of Southern universities." This includes not only the monument, but also the name of the university's athletic teams, the "Ole Miss Rebels."

Whether one talks about the meanings of the two world wars for Hungarian identity or, in our own case, the meaning of the struggles of 1861–65 — and, of course, what we call that struggle, whether Civil War, War between the States, a War for (or to Suppress) Southern Independence, or an insurrection, is scarcely an innocent choice — they are essentially contested. Partisans on all sides proclaim, perhaps even accurately, that nothing less than the national culture is at stake, especially insofar as material representations of such events, such as monuments or even street names and the like — the Jefferson Davis Highway remains a central connector between Washington, D.C., and Richmond, Virginia — are thought to play some role in inculcating particular understandings of society within future generations.

One manifestation of this contest concerns the control of "sacred space."[8] Such space is exemplified for Americans by the National Mall in Washington — described by one historian, objecting to the proposed location of a new monument honoring the veterans of World War II, as "the most precious plot of ground in the country . . .

our most sacred space"[9]—public cemeteries, state and national capitol grounds, and other ground that is invested with special meaning within the structure of the civil religion that helps to constitute a given social order. Or the space can be more obviously metaphorical, as with the design of flags, the declaration of public holidays, such as Martin Luther King's birthday, or even the designation of official state songs. As to this last, for example, Virginia has recently retired its state song, "Carry Me Back to Old Virginia." Composed by James A. Bland, a black minstrel from New York, it is written from the perspective of a Virginia-loving freed slave whose fondest wish, apparently, is to be reunited after his death with his beloved "massa and missis." Contemporary Virginians have decided that it is time for this evocation of "Old Virginia" to leave the stage, to be replaced, one presumes, by a song more congruent with the social realities of the contemporary commonwealth.

Sacred grounds characteristically serve as venues for public art, including monuments to social heroes. Yet a sometimes bitter reality about life within truly multicultural societies is that the very notion of a unified public is up for grabs. As already suggested, one aspect of multiculturalism is precisely that different cultures are likely to have disparate—and even conflicting—notions of who counts as heroes or villains. And, as we shall see below, the debate over the fate of the Liberty Monument in New Orleans is now in at least its third decade. The reason why the debate continues, rather than being settled, is precisely that we are a multicultural society wrestling with the question how, if at all, one produces *unum* out of the *pluribus* of American society.

The section below offers some reflections on the role of public art within the social order, with specific reference to memorialization of the events of 1861–65. Perhaps because my principal identity is as a constitutional lawyer, I go on to ask if the United States Constitution offers any aid in resolving the sometimes volatile controversies generated by memorialization. I well recognize, though, that whatever one's answer about the importance of specifically legal argument, that no society lives by law alone, and I go on to discuss how we ought to respond to certain complaints even if the law properly does not compel a given resolution.

Public Art and the Constitution of Social Meaning

Art has many functions, only some of which can be reduced to learning to appreciate standard aesthetic criteria of beauty and form. Art is, among other things, both the terrain of, and often a weapon in, the culture wars that course through societies. This is, of course, especially true of public art—the art chosen self-consciously by public institutions to symbolize the public order and to inculcate in its viewers appropriate attitudes toward that order. Although occasional museum curators may devote themselves to "art for art's sake," I think it fair to say that this concept makes no sense to anyone concerned with the art that is found in those spaces that are most truly "public" in a political sense, such as the space surrounding capitol buildings, city halls, national cemeteries, and the like. Art placed within those spaces is almost always the product of some instrumental purpose outside the domain of pure aesthetics, and one's analysis (or response) to such art will inevitably be influenced by knowledge about its topical subject and the political resonance that surrounds it. One might, I suppose, deny the honorific "art" to such cre- ations, but I am not sure what purpose that denial would serve, especially given that great museums all over the world are filled with objects whose original purpose was to serve political ends and whose formal aesthetic merits may sometimes be questionable.

As already noted, I am interested primarily in Southern cities and their use of public space. I thus begin with Richmond, Virginia, and its aptly named Monument Avenue, one of its principal thoroughfares. It gains its name from the fact that over many blocks one sees impressive statues of Confederate leaders, including Jefferson Davis, the President of the Confederate States of America, and three of his most prominent generals, J. E. B. Stuart, Stonewall Jackson, and, of course, Robert E. Lee. A final statue memorializes Matthew Fontaine Maury, "the father of modern oceanography" who resigned his commission in the United States Navy to command, albeit from the shore (because of an injury), the naval forces of the Confederacy.

From Monument Avenue in Richmond, Virginia: Jefferson Davis (above), Robert E. Lee (above right), Stonewall Jackson (right), J. E. B. Stuart (facing page, left), and Matthew Fontaine Maury (facing page, right) (photos by John Paul Jones).

It perhaps goes without saying that there is no memorial to Abraham Lincoln or to Ulysses S. Grant on Monument Avenue or, so far as I know, elsewhere in Richmond. Michael Kammen laconically notes that a 1902 effort by some Confederate veterans to erect a memorial to Grant in Richmond foundered after receiving only sixteen dollars! And consider this outraged response by President Lyon G. Tyler of William and Mary to a 1908 proposal to erect a statue to Lincoln:

> To ask the South to put a monument to Lincoln, who represents Northern invasion of the homes and firesides of the South, would be as absurd as if I were to ask the North to put up a

monument to Jefferson Davis. . . . I do not care to force [Davis's] memory upon a people with whom he is not identified. In the same way, I am sure that the South can never be brought to regard Mr. Lincoln in any other political light than that in which Mr. Davis is regarded by the North—as the champion of a section.[10]

Although one might be forgiven the surmise that Lee and Davis are unmemorialized in any Northern city, a monument to Lee was erected at the Gettysburg battle-field in 1917, upon the initial sponsorship of Virginia and Pennsylvania in 1903, just as a monument to the Confederate dead had been unveiled at Arlington National Cemetery in 1914. These were scarcely uncontroversial. Edward Linenthal notes an 1887 vote by the national encampment of posts of the Grand Army of the Republic "that no local post should support 'erection of monuments in honor of men who distinguished themselves by their services in the cause of treason and rebellion,' "[11] and the G.A.R. successfully blocked Virginia's attempt to place Lee in the statuary hall of the United States Capitol. For better or worse, such passions had presumably dissipated thirty years later, as charges of "treason and rebellion" were forgotten and replaced by new narratives of the courage and valor displayed by adherents of the Lost Cause now joined together with their former opponents in an ever-more-truly *United* States.

The most notable tribute to Lincoln is obviously found some 120 miles north of Richmond, in Washington, D.C. The Lincoln Memorial is the central temple of the American civil religion, though smaller memorials to the sixteenth President dot especially the Northern and Midwestern landscape. One can, of course, find jointly shared heroes of the two cultures, the most obvious one being George Washington, venerated both in Richmond and the city that bears his name. (Though recall that the current New Orleans school board refuses to honor Washington at all, given his status as a slaveholder.) Consider, however, the fact that the great obelisk called the Washington Monument is surrounded by American flags and is clearly meant to celebrate Washington the national liberator, the founding father of a new Union, not Washington the Virginian. One doubts that this is altogether true of the Houdon statue of Washington in Richmond, whose local admirers might want us to believe that Washington, like Robert E. Lee, would have given priority to his Virginia identity over his national one had the two ever emerged sharply in conflict in his own lifetime. After all, Washington had given priority to his parochial American identity against wider loyalties to the Great Britain that claimed sovereign authority over its colonies.

Moving farther south, to Columbia, South Carolina, one can see not only civil statuary reminiscent of Richmond's (though nowhere so grandly displayed as on Monument Avenue), but also, waving over the state capitols (though under the American flag), the battle flag of the Confederate States of America to which South Carolina, like Virginia, proudly belonged (or, depending on one's theory, attempted to belong) between 1861–65. This flag, the "Southern Cross," is commonly, though incorrectly referred to as the "Stars and Bars," which properly refers to the "official" flag of the Confederate States of America, which consisted of three stripes—two red separated by a white—and a circle of seven stars in the upper corner.

Most Americans, one suspects, could not identify this official flag, whereas few indeed, whatever their regional background, could fail to identify the battle flag. This no doubt helps to explain why the state flags of Georgia and Mississippi explicitly incorporate the battle flag of the Confederacy, rather than the official flag, into their current state flags.

One quite dramatic difference, then, between many Eastern European capitals and those of the present United States is precisely the extent to which memorials to lost (and ostensibly defeated) causes continue to occupy places of public honor. Unlike the displaced statues of Stalin or Hoxha, the statues on Monument Avenue (and elsewhere throughout the South) remain for all to see (and learn from). Since 1884, for example, visitors to New Orleans have been able to see a statue of Robert E. Lee rising high above the landscape, and even the buildings of modern New Orleans have not entirely diminished its power at the center of Lee Circle.

Far more startling to a contemporary consciousness is another New Orleans monument, this one erected in 1891 commemorating the so-called Battle of Liberty Place, an 1874 encounter in downtown New Orleans.[12] An admiring local historian describes the battle as "The Overthrow of Carpet-Bag Rule in New Orleans—September 14, 1874," and he is clearly not alone in his feelings about the battle. An extensive review of the event in a 1920 issue of the *Louisiana Historical Quarterly* concludes as follows:

> Well may New Orleans glory in its Liberty Monument, for it commemorates a wonderful page in its history; but not much less distinct should be the pride therein of all the people of this great country, for it tells of the binding up of old wounds and of the cementing of ties, that have enabled this nation of ours to grow and prosper and to become, as it is today, a worthy example to all the world.

The denizens being honored were members of the aptly named White League, who engaged in the violent overthrow of the existing Louisiana government, composed of an alliance of Republican whites and newly enfranchised African Americans. Thirty-two lives were lost on both sides, with about three times that many persons injured. The ousted administration of the Republican William Penn Kellogg was in fact restored by force of federal arms, but it was only a matter of time until the Compromise of 1877

The Liberty Monument, as of 1996, removed from its previous setting at the base of Canal Street in New Orleans.

resulted in the full-scale restoration of conservative white rule sought by the White League, with attendant consequences for the future of African Americans.

Immediately following the battle, with the partisans of the White League in apparent control of the state (of which New Orleans was then the capital), the *New Orleans Daily Picayune* saluted the downfall of the former government. "Big, inflated, insolent, and overbearing, it collapsed at one touch of honest indignation and gallant onslaught." This leading voice of New Orleans called for the erection of a memorial to the eleven whites who had died on behalf of the insurgency. The New Orleans City Council formally agreed in November 1882, when it passed an ordinance renaming the area of the battle as "Liberty Place" and authorized the erection of a monument "in honor of those who fell in defense of liberty and home rule in that heroic struggle of the 14th of September, 1874." By 1891 these hopes were achieved with the construction of an obelisk near the Mississippi River at the foot of Canal Street, a principal thoroughfare in the city. The Liberty Monument included the names of those White Leaguers who gave their lives in attacking the hated mixed-race government, as well as the names of some of the League leaders. It goes almost without saying that the members of the Metropolitan Police and of the largely black militia who died fighting the White League were unmemorialized. The 1891 dedication of the monument apparently initiated what became a yearly parade thereafter on each September 14th, with suitable wreath-laying ceremonies to honor the civic heroes.

Lest anyone fail to get the intended message, the city, using artisans funded by the New Deal's Work Projects Administration, added in 1934 two plaques setting out what might be called, in our postmodernist times, the officially privileged narrative of the events. On one side of the base was chiseled, "United States troops took over the state government and reinstated the usurpers but the national election in November 1876 recognized white supremacy and gave us our state." On the opposite side appeared, "McEnery and Penn, having been elected governor and lieutenant governor by the white people, were duly installed by the overthrow of the carpetbag government, ousting the usurpers Gov. Kellogg (white) and Lt. Gov. Antoine (colored)."

As one might well expect, the Liberty Monument has remained a source of controversy in New Orleans, especially as African Americans have become a dominant political force in the city (though no one should confuse this with a genuine regime change à la Hungary). In 1974, for example, Mayor Moon Landrieu agreed to the installation of a bronze plaque describing the battle as an insurrection and noting that the controversial language had not in fact been part of the original 1891 monument. Most important, no doubt, was the plaque's additional message that "the sentiments expressed are contrary to the philosophy and beliefs of present-day New Orleans," a statement itself raising delicious political and philosophical questions. Is New Orleans an entity that can have a "philosophy and beliefs," and, if so, how precisely does one identify what they are? Who is granted the power to speak authoritatively as to their content? One might well believe, of course, that the statement was designed more to *create* a desired state of public consciousness than to describe accurately the actual constellation of public opinion in New Orleans as of 1974. Still, there can be no doubt that New Orleans adopted an overtly tutelary role in attempting to limit the pernicious consequences upon the untutored who might otherwise have been tempted to treat the words contained on the monument—and placed there, after all, at public expense—as an authoritative enunciation of the meaning of the commemorated event.

When Ernest Morial became the first black mayor of the city in 1981, he attempted to remove the monument but was stopped from doing so by the majority-white city council, which forbade the moving of any monuments without its consent. The council did, however, authorize the removal of any offensive wording on the monument. Smooth granite slabs were then placed over the 1934 additions, presumably obviating the need for the adjoining plaque's renunciatory sentiments. During the late 1980s the administration of a second black mayor, Sidney Barthelemy, tried to remove the monument permanently during the course of general riverfront reconstruction, when it had been taken down temporarily from its Canal Street location. However, an interesting alliance of traditionalists, historical preservationists, and white supremacists successfully blocked the effort. Nevertheless, the monument was ultimately moved from its quite prominent Canal Street spot to a decidedly more obscure setting about a block away, where it now languishes out of the sight of most of the tourists who otherwise crowd Canal Street and its fine shops, casinos, the municipal aquarium, and vistas of the Mississippi. It remains in the general area only because of a consent agreement between the city and the Louisiana State Historic Preservation Officer, based on federal historic preservation laws, that the monument remain in the general area of the battle.

Once again, though, the official narrative changed, as yet another large plaque was placed on the monument itself. It contained the names of the eleven members of the Metropolitan Police who lost their lives in the conflict. More important, for our purposes, is the new official message of the Monument: "IN HONOR OF THOSE AMERICANS ON BOTH SIDES OF THE CONFLICT WHO DIED IN THE BATTLE OF LIBERTY PLACE. A CONFLICT OF THE PAST THAT SHOULD TEACH US LESSONS FOR THE FUTURE." What these lessons might be is left wholly unarticulated. The voice of the tutor is quite muffled, leaving the monument to speak for itself without further elaboration. If the Millennium Monument evokes Musil's *Man Without Qualities,* this latest inscription on the Liberty Monument brings to mind either George Orwell, with his castigation of government doubletalk, or, perhaps

SEPTEMBER 14TH 1874
IN HONOR OF THOSE AMERICANS
ON BOTH SIDES OF THE CONFLICT
WHO DIED IN THE BATTLE OF LIBERTY PLACE
MEMBERS OF THE METROPOLITAN POLICE
JOHN H.H. CAMP
J.F. CLERMONT
DAVID FISHER
ARMSTED HILL
JOHN KENNEDY
J.E. KOEHLER
JAMES McMANUS
MICHAEL O'KEEFE
EDWARD SIMON
WILLIAM THORNTON
RUDOLPHE ZIPPLE
A CONFLICT OF THE PAST
THAT SHOULD TEACH US LESSONS FOR THE FUTURE

The Liberty Monument.

less ominously, Sir Arthur Strebe-Greebling (a character created by the late comedian Peter Cook), who unforgettably stated, "Oh yes, I've learned from my mistakes and I'm sure I could repeat them exactly." One wonders if this present inscription on the Liberty Monument genuinely represents progress over the 1974 point and counterpoint that at least educated the careful reader in the ideological stakes behind the ascription of meaning to the Liberty Monument.

Similarly, the Confederate flag continues to fly over some official buildings — and to plague contemporary politics — after the hammer and sickle has become but a memory (or, at least, been reduced to an object of flag-waving protest by private individuals dismayed by the sea change that has occurred since 1991). Many Southerners, in particular, would gladly echo the comment of Theodore Herzl, one of the founders of Zionism:

> You might ask mockingly: "A flag? What's that? A stick with a rag on it?" No sir, a flag is much more. With a flag you lead men, for a flag, men live and die. In fact, it is the only thing for which they are ready to die in masses, if you train them for it. Believe me, the politics of an entire people . . . can be manipulated only through the imponderables that float in the air.[13]

Even Georgia's popular Governor Zell Miller was unable to prevail in his efforts to change the flag back to the pre-

1956 Georgia emblem, which, ironically, is different from the current flag only insofar as the earlier emblem was apparently modeled after the official Confederate flag—the historic "Stars and Bars"—rather than the crossed lines of stars of the battle flag. And the newly elected Republican attorney general of South Carolina in 1994 reversed the policy of his Democratic predecessor by announcing that he would defend against a lawsuit challenging the right of the state to continue flying the Confederate battle flag atop the South Carolina statehouse. And we saw above the uncertain response to South Carolina Governor Beasley's more recent attempt to lower the flag.

I offer one final example of public sculpture, a monument found in front of the Texas state capitol in Austin. The approximately twenty-feet-high statue is the first thing the visitor entering the south capitol grounds will see, even before the monument celebrating the defenders of the Alamo. Erected in 1903 by their "surviving comrades" in the John B. Hood Camp, United Confederate Veterans, it commemorates those who died fighting for the Confederacy between 1861–65. On a pedestal stand seven-foot statues of an artilleryman, an infantryman, a cavalryman, and a sailor, representing the four branches of the Confederate armed forces. Rising from the center of the pedestal is a seven-and-one-half-feet-tall statue of Jefferson Davis. According to the contemporary state librarian who compiled a breathless history of the monument, the viewer "will instinctively look up at the commanding, heroic form above

Memorial to the Confederate Dead, state capitol grounds, Austin, Texas.

him, a personification of the Genius of the Confederacy, its faith, its intelligence, its enlightened appreciation and love of liberty, its lofty purpose, its dauntless courage, and its inflexible iron will." [14] On the side of the top pedestal is a listing of each of the Confederate states (plus Missouri and Kentucky, two of the Unionist slave states).

Lower down, on three of the monument's sides, are carved the names of every battle fought during the four-year carnage. On the fourth side appears the official message of the monument:

DIED FOR STATE RIGHTS

GUARANTEED UNDER THE CONSTITUTION

THE PEOPLE OF THE SOUTH, ANIMATED BY THE SPIRIT OF 1776, TO PRESERVE THEIR RIGHTS, WITHDREW FROM THE FEDERAL COMPACT IN 1861. THE NORTH RESORTED TO COERCION. THE SOUTH, AGAINST OVER-WHELMING NUMBERS AND RESOURCES, FOUGHT UNTIL EXHAUSTED.*

The monument is dated 1901, though it seems not to have been completed until 1903, when it was formally unveiled and dedicated on April 16. An onlooker described the dedication speeches, first of former Governor Lubbock, who had been an aide to Davis, and then of Texas' current Governor Lanham: Lubbock was "delighted to see the grand work of perpetuating the Confederacy. . . . He declared one thing which grates on his ear is to hear someone say that we fought for what we considered was right. 'We fought for what we know was right,' declared

*One might compare this inscription with that found on monument to the Union dead located in the Boston Common: To the Men of Boston / Who Died for their country / On Land and Sea in the War / Which Kept the Union Whole / Destroyed Slavery / And Maintained the Constitution / The Grateful City Has Built this Monument / That Their Example May Speak to Coming Generations.

Monument to the Union Dead, Boston Common.

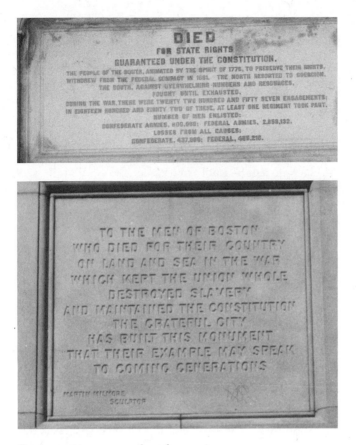

*Two competing messages about the meaning
of the war and of the lives lost.*

the speaker." As Governor Lanham spoke, he "pointed directly at the statue of President Davis, and eloquently exclaimed, 'I salute thee!'" and then saluted the statues of the four soldiers. According to the *Austin Daily Statesman*, this "brought forth a mighty shout of applause from those present," as did the governor's declaration "that, if he ever heard any one abusing President Davis or the noble cause he championed, he would first remonstrate with him, and if that did not suffice, he would feel sorely tempted to strike the offenders with a shillalah."

I have been fascinated by the monument since discovering it shortly after moving to Austin. I include its "message" in the casebook, *Processes of Constitutional Decisionmaking,* that I coedit, and I usually devote a class to assessing the interpretation of the Constitution that it offers. *Can* one describe the people of the South as simply engaging in their right of self-determination, as set out in the Declaration of Independence and, perhaps, implicitly guaranteed by the Tenth Amendment to the United States Constitution as a reserved right to revert to their sovereign power to secede from the United States and forge a new path in a different political setting? This also requires asking if it is truly thinkable that one might describe Abraham Lincoln, the cult figure of our national civil religion, as an illegitimate coercer, perhaps similar to George III (not to mention more ominous twentieth-century nationalists who have refused to let dissident, regionally organized, minorities go in peace).

I certainly do not want to argue that the monument's view of secession is the only legitimate view. I am willing, though, to proffer a defense of the legitimacy of secession as a general proposition of normative political theory; perhaps more to the point, I am also willing to defend its plausibility even within our particular political system. I do not think it is impossible to interpret the Constitution as allowing secession even within the United States, at least if carried out with full popular deliberation and consent of those doing the seceding. Like Confederate Vice-President Alexander Stephens, I believe that Abraham Lincoln had more than a trace of "union mysticism" that led him to underestimate the theoretical force of the Southern argument for voluntary dissolution of the Union.

At this point, though, one might protest that the discussion is turning "academic" in the pejorative sense. After all, can one really maintain a stance of academic distance in discussing the legitimacy of the secessionist movements of 1860–61? One reason for our skepticism is that we are talking about our very own country, whose identity has been profoundly shaped precisely by the national decision, purchased between 1861 and 1865 by the lifeblood of one of every fifty Americans, to reject the possibility of secession. It is a bit like trying to analyze dispassionately whether our own parents really should have married one another; perhaps, after all, they were unsuited to each other and would have been happier had they never met. The one thing we know for sure about any such counterfactual possibility, whatever consequences it might have had for our parents, is that we would not exist with the specific identity that constitutes whatever individuality we possess. Similarly, it is truly impossible to imagine what our political identity would be like had the separations of 1861 stuck. For those of us who take politics — and identity — seriously, that is an important consideration.

But even these musings remain much too abstract, an almost obvious attempt to evade what for most of us is the overwhelming reality of the events of 1861–65. Along with discussion of the high theory of sovereignty, popular and otherwise, one must attend to the reality of the chattel slavery that certainly exemplified the greatest difference between North and South and explained much of the impetus for national dissolution. Indeed, for me the reality of slavery provides the only justification for the suppression of the Southern effort to gain political independence.

If partisans of Lincoln's policy tend to focus on slavery to the exclusion of the abstract merits of arguments in behalf of secession, so do those who defend the Lost Cause tend to emphasize only the latter while ignoring the most ignominious realities of the Southern way of life. Thus, those who designed the Texas statue and its inscription were conforming to what the historian Gaines Foster has described as the standard line adopted by Confederate memorializers, who insisted that the Southern cause had been just and legal, with "Confederate armies [having] fought not for slavery but for constitutional rights, the principle of secession, and the preservation of their homeland." The Texans were also altogether typical in ascribing the loss to the result of the "overwhelming numbers" of Northern troops rather than, for example, to Confederate shortcomings. The spirit of the statue is aptly captured in the comment of an ex-Confederate soldier, quoted by Foster, upon the occasion of a reunion at Gettysburg that was addressed by the first Southern president elected since 1848, Woodrow Wilson. This former Confederate proudly proclaimed that Southern veterans presented "no apology, no explanation, no expression of regret, no humiliation, no retraction, no recanting." [15]

Whatever one's views on the theoretical merits of secession and self-determination, they must always be tempered by recognition of the particular context within which a secessionist argument is being made, whether in South Carolina in 1861 or in Bosnia in 1995. And that context, so far as the United States is concerned, includes, overwhelmingly, slavery and state political systems devoted to maintaining what was euphemistically called our "peculiar institution." Thus one must always ask if a monument to the Confederate dead—and the articulation of secessionist constitutional theory—is equivalent to memorializing those who fought to maintain chattel slavery and the abuse of African Americans. And, if so, does this mean, like medieval suicides, that those who died in that fight should be denied the consecrated burial in sacred soil that is symbolized by the monument? (Indeed, this is one of three monuments to

Confederate veterans found on the Texas capitol grounds, though it is certainly the largest and most visible.)

Consider the German cemetery at Bitburg, with its graves and, more importantly, memorial tombstones to members of the SS. For many of us, the lowest symbolic point of the Reagan presidency was his capitulation to Chancellor Kohl's desire that the president of the United States in effect offer these Nazi war criminals the symbolic absolution of his charismatic presence at their gravesites. Ian Buruma, in his superb book *Wages of Guilt,* about the German and Japanese cultural responses to World War II, notes that there were, after World War I, many *Denkmale,* war memorials celebrating the sacrifices of German soldiers. Unsurprisingly, this did not occur following 1945; instead one sees *Mahnmale,* memorials to the victims of Hitlerian Germany. "The warning monuments and memorial places (*Gedenkstatte*) are mostly products of the reaction, which set in during the 1960s, propelled by the postwar generation, as eager to warn and remember as their parents were to forget." Bitburg was a manifestation, if not of a desire to forget, at least of a desire in some ways to normalize the experience of fighting on behalf of the German state between 1939–45. It was, perhaps, the ultimate repudiation of the ban, until the 1950s, on building military cemeteries, a ban that was coupled with the pulling down, by the occupying Allies, of many of their older memorials that commemorated the Prussian military tradition.

To the extent that we credit even the slightest equivalence to these comparisons, or to earlier implicit comparisons between the Old South and the Soviet Union, then what ought we do today in regard to statues like the one in Austin, not to mention those that line Monument Avenue or the streets of New Orleans? Do the newly empowered citizens of Moscow and St. Petersburg provide role models of how to respond to offensive public sculpture that owes its genesis to the attempt of a specific sociopolitical regime to reinforce its dominion and promote a particular kind of political consciousness? After all, as Kirk Savage reminds us, "Public monuments do not arise as if by natural law to celebrate the deserving; they are built by people with sufficient power to marshal (or impose) public consent for their erection." A "public monument represents a kind of collective recognition—in short, legitimacy—for the memory deposited there."[16] Once one recognizes this basic truth, then it surely seems possible to argue that at least some sculpture, whatever its aesthetic merits or utility as an example of how material artifacts are used to constitute a culture, properly faces destruction as the penalty for its association with a hated political regime. Is there any merit to the suggestion that this is just the kind of destruction of historical memory that bespeaks the totalitarian impulse and should be resisted even (or especially) when its claims seem most compelling?

There are, to be sure, intermediate solutions. During the period of maximum controversy within New Orleans about the fate of the Liberty Monument, the noted Yale historian Robin Winks attacked those who counseled its destruction.[17] He took direct issue with those who viewed the struggle over its appropriateness as a public monument as a "clash between those who look to the future and those who hang on to the past, or even more sharply put, between racists and those who regard race as irrelevant." Instead, he opined, the struggle is really about the nature of historical memory. "Different concepts of history are at war." The first "holds that society should never forget any part of its past," that "it is wrong to purge the record" of past events. Winks evoked the classic negative example of the justly derided "Great Soviet Encyclopedia," which was subject to constant revisions based on the ideological desires of those ruling at any given instant. "History became what the written texts said it was" instead of a rendering of history as it actually happened.

But Winks is much too sophisticated to stay with this polarized opposition. "We all know," he writes, that "history is, simultaneously, three things: what actually happened, what historians choose to record, and what the people—and people, some people, these people, those people—believe to be true about the past." Were he writing for a more academic audience, he might well have segued into a language about the existence of competing discourses that compete for cultural hegemony and whose partisans attempt, by use of the state apparatus, to privilege. He might also have contrasted the versions of history predominant within the academy, at any given point, with those held by the untutored or, perhaps more precisely, those who accept as their tutors uncertified amateurs instead of the credentialed academy. It was just such a struggle between professional historians and the untutored (other than by their own experiences) populace that was at the center of the struggle over the exhibition of the Enola Gay, the plane from which the Hiroshima atomic bomb was dropped, at the National Air and Space Museum in 1995, the fiftieth anniversary of end of World War II. It was altogether appropriate that the editors of a series of essays on the controversy titled their book *History Wars: The* Enola Gay *and Other Battles for the American Past.*

"The past," Winks points out, "is also what is commemorated by monuments and markers, plaques and parades, historic sites and museums. Almost always a monument is an attempt to interpret an event in which those who have erected it take pride." They are ways by which a specific culture names its heroes, those "people who made us what we are in a prideful way." There is, I believe, a linkage between Winks's comment and Catharine MacKinnon's argument, expressed in somewhat more radical language:

> Words and images are how people are placed
> in hierarchies, how social stratification is made
> to seem inevitable and right, how feelings of
> inferiority and superiority are engendered, and
> how indifference to violence against those on the

bottom is rationalized and normalized. Social supremacy is made, inside and between people, through making meanings.[18]

So what we have is a monument whose origin was the desire to honor those who took up arms against a multi-racial government and whose present meaning (even 120 years later) for many is to pay homage to the racist culture for which they fought. Though even here a cautionary note may be necessary. Thus University of Texas professor of literature (and poet and Jungian depth psychologist) Betty Sue Flowers contends:

> Surely the "desire"—insofar as we can claim to know—was to honor those who fought for the right to a representative government. It's easy to get a mob to ignite against a "multi-racial government"—but to get a sustained fundraising effort going, you have to have a principle at work rather than simply a prejudice. The principle in this case was connected (in the [white] Southerners' minds at least) to the reason they came to America in the first place. In the carpet-bagger governments set up, they had no vote; their property was often confiscated, etc., etc. I think you have to take seriously the stated reason for the "honor" bestowed on the fallen—they fought for "liberty and home rule." Were

they also anti-black racists? Yes. But the *meaning* of the statue must surely take into account the point of view of these Southerners as well as our more enlightened one.

Whatever the importance of Flowers's reminder, it is worth noting that some supporters of the monument, like the Louisiana White Citizens Council, essentially agree with opponents like the local NAACP that the central purpose of the monument is to celebrate those who took arms against the Reconstruction government—save only, one presumes, by the refusal on the part of the former to describe the ancien régime as racist. So if one rejects the Citizens Council and the White League that was in a significant sense its predecessor, why not emulate the Russians in tearing the monument down and proclaiming through the very act of destruction the commitment to a new, and presumably better, vision of reality?

Winks demurs. "The monument must go back up." Escalating his rhetoric and adopting what is surely among the most censurious epithets in an intellectual's vocabulary, he says that "not to put it back up would be an act of the clearest Stalinism, of intellectual vandalism." Interestingly, though, this scarcely concludes Winks's discussion. For him the real issue is not whether to keep it standing but, rather, *where* to place the statue. He agrees that it is not appropriate to keep it near its historic Canal Street setting, whatever the arguments of the historic preservationists. There it serves primarily as "an insult to most of the present population of New Orleans, . . . rub[bing] salt in open wounds not yet healed," and a decent political order can presumably act to remove the source of such hurt, to silence the message it sends.

What, then, is Winks's solution? It is to encapsulate the monument within a museum, where it presumably takes on a different semiotic status. In some museums the new status would be that of "aesthetic object," in which form is substantially separated from content. But no one defends the totally undistinguished Liberty Monument as art. So the museum being referred to is one devoted particularly to history. And the message, presumably, is that the object in question is now safely displaced to the past, at some distance — both emotional and intellectual — from the exigencies of the present. Winks offers the example of Zimbabwe, which, upon its creation as the successor-state to Rhodesia, was faced with the issue of what to do with the "great statues of Cecil Rhodes, Lord Salisbury and others who dreamt of empire" that filled "the central squares of [Rhodesia's capital] Salisbury." "Of course the new civil servants of Zimbabwe did not wish to walk past larger-than-life figures of Cecil Rhodes or Lord Salisbury as they went to their new jobs." They did not, however, destroy the statues or otherwise "deny the significance of Cecil Rhodes to the history of modern Zimbabwe." Instead, they moved the statues from the great public spaces of the city "and carefully and skillfully put them once again on the grounds of the nation's new national archives and museum, a clear statement that the figure spoke to the past, not to the future."

Presumably the movement of the statues, together with the change of the country's name itself and its capital's name from Salisbury to Harare, served to secularize them, turning them into detached objects of historical reflection rather than icons of an ongoing civil religion. Moreover, I strongly suspect that not all of the memorials to Rhodes and Salisbury were moved to historical museums. There were undoubtedly too many of them; this was clearly the case in the former Soviet Union, where far more statues of Lenin had been produced than could possibly be absorbed by museums. So, presumably, most of the statues were destroyed even if the aesthetically best, or most publicly prominent, individual statues were given a type of immortal life in museums.

Even if one agrees with Winks that complete destruction of these monuments is unwise, whether or not "Stalinist," one might obviously wonder if the state should be content to count on the placement within a museum setting to convey the proper message. Even if this removes some of the force that placement in sacred space gives any statue, it scarcely offers a complete resolution for the dilemma, for those particular state employees called museum curators must still decide how, precisely, they should be presented within the museum setting. Perhaps the museum should play a much more active tutelary role in setting out the

The entrance to Statue Park, Budapest, Hungary (1997).

moral it wishes those viewing the statues to draw. For the state to profess to be truly neutral or indifferent to the social meaning of given statuary would be not only remarkable (assuming, of course, it is possible), it might also, under many circumstances, be pernicious.

I presume that Winks would counsel that the new government of South Africa follow the Zimbabwean example of keeping in place public monuments to oppressors. Afrikaaners should presumably still be able to see mighty monuments to their ancestors, though in museums rather than at great public squares. Perhaps one would similarly advise the new governments of Russia, Poland, and other countries formerly ruled by Communists to place various statues of Lenin, Stalin, and others in the equivalent of Communist theme parks, where parents could bring their children and impart whatever lessons they wished. This has happened in contemporary Budapest, where one can find Statue Park Museum on the outskirts of the city. One enters the park through a suitably imposing facade, which reveals the statues sitting in a field.

As a guidebook to the park explains, "Here gathered together are all the statues of Budapest that once stood in public places, as beacons for the political and ideological culture of the former socialist period." The architect of the park, Akos Eleod, noted that he tried his "utmost to treat this terribly serious theme with the proper amount of

Communist statues in Budapest, Hungary (1997).

Commemoration of the Soviet liberators of Budapest from the Nazis: This is the only remaining Communist statue in public Budapest.

seriousness," but this was no easy matter. "I had to realise that if I constructed this park with more tendentious, extreme or realistic methods . . . I would ultimately be doing nothing more than constructing my own Anti-propaganda park from these propagandist statues, and following the same thought patterns and prescriptions of dictatorship that erected these statues in the first place." Thus the park, "about dictatorship," is "at the same time . . . about democracy. After all, only democracy is able to give the opportunity to let us think freely about dictatorship."

Only one Communist monument remains in the city itself, a memorial to the Soviet soldiers who died liberating Budapest from the Nazis in 1945. Opposite the American embassy in one of Budapest's principal public squares, it remains, red star and all, in part because a number of the soldiers slain during the liberation are buried beneath it. (One of the wonderfully rich experiences of contemporary Budapest is to place the unpretentious memorial to the slain Imre Nagy in the same sightline as the imposing monument to the Soviet soldiers.)

Would we have found the Budapest solution acceptable in Germany and Japan following their defeats in World War II? Surely most of us would have been profoundly dissatisfied had the successor regimes moved any public statuary of Hitler, Tojo, and their minions to the carefully tended grounds of a state museum where they would stand, without further adornment or explanation, for the presumed edification of onlookers. Postmodernist irony would scarcely have seemed a sufficient response to the horrors of the Nazis (which suggests that, in spite of everything, the Communist rule is treated as far less loathsome than the Nazi hegemony).

Similar questions can be asked in regard to public display of the flag. It is truly impossible to believe that the Russia is under some duty to maintain the hammer and

The Memorial to Imre Nagy, executed by the Communists in the aftermath of 1956 and now portrayed as glancing over his shoulder to the parliament building a block away.

sickle as its national symbol, or that the swastika should have been kept as a part of the German flag? I presume that no one finds morally innocent the waving of the swastika by contemporary skinheads in Germany or other countries. Imagine our reaction if a German *staat,* perhaps inspired by South Carolina, decided to fly the swastika above its state capitol. Does our reaction to these flags suggest anything at all in regard to the Confederate flag and its distinctive set of associations?

The Fourteenth Amendment,
State Speech, and Public Symbols

What stance should we take regarding those who wish to tear down (or maintain) monuments and other historical artifacts? Can we construct some general theoretical positions that will provide answers to the conundrums facing us, or, on the contrary, is each situation so context-dependent that generalizations get us nowhere? One is reminded of Justice Stewart's famous statement about the possibility of developing a general definition of pornography. He could not, he said, come up with such a definition, but did say, "I know it when I see it." Similarly, it is possible that we cannot agree on a general approach to the problems presented by public homage, but, nonetheless, regarding acceptability, "we know it when we see it."

As a constitutional lawyer, I am particularly interested in whether legal analysis is helpful in approaching such questions. Law is certainly the most systematic attempt to provide high-level, generalized, rules for covering complex social conflicts. It is tempting, therefore, to ask if the United States Constitution speaks with enough clarity to invalidate the display of the Confederate battle flag or the raising of certain monuments, at least when done by state officials. Consider a Texan who claims that the presence of the statue in front of the capitol is not only personally offensive, which could certainly be the case, but also a violation of his or her constitutional rights. Or a Georgian asserts similar claims regarding the Georgia state flag, redesigned by the Georgia Legislature—to add the Confederate battle flag, which now covers roughly two-thirds of the flag's area—only in 1956 as an expression of disdain for the Supreme Court's decision in *Brown v. Board of Education.* What arguments for their illegality, at least as explicitly public symbols, might be made and, more importantly, accepted?

It must be noted that, whatever else may be said about flags atop state capitols (and about most public art), there is no need to dispute this as an action of the state and thus subject to constitutional constraint. Many of the debates about the Confederate flag have concerned its display by private persons and their rights under the First Amendment to be protected against state interference in the expression of their views, however obnoxious the form of that expression might be. As a long-time card-carrying member of the American Civil Liberties Union, I have no trouble protecting such display, not least because I do not trust the state to make refined judgments as to whose symbols are sufficiently obnoxious to merit criminal punishment. But public entities have no rights to free speech as such, nor are we talking of "criminalizing" the speech of the reified State.

A moment's reflection should make clear that certain speech that is almost absolutely protected when uttered by ordinary individuals—e.g., "You ought to accept Jesus Christ as your Lord and Savior"—is clearly unconstitutional when presented by the state as official public policy. But why would that expression be unconstitutional? The answer is almost certainly not because it gives offense to non-Christians or exemplifies a Christian hegemony that has often had the most deleterious consequences for non-Christians, however important those facts are as a practical matter. Rather, the invalidity, at least under conventional legal analysis, is the consequence of the meaning given a patch of constitutional text, the First Amendment, that explicitly bans the establishment of religion. This is cor- rectly interpreted to prohibit, among other things, the endorsement by the state of specific theological views. The question is whether there is a way of reading the Confederate flag or a Confederate public monument to include it within the universe of state declarations that the Constitution, correctly interpreted, prohibits.

The quixotic quest for "neutrality" in public space

One might try to answer this question by adopting the language of neutrality that is so influential in regard to religion. Thus the Supreme Court has stated, in one of its foundational Establishment Clause cases, that the Constitution means not only that the state cannot "set up a church," but also, and, in practical effect, more significantly, that it also cannot "pass laws which aid one religion, aid all religions, or prefer one religion over another." That is, the state must be relentlessly neutral, neither favoring nor burdening any given religious view or even the view that religion, in some general sense, is to be preferred to irreligion.

Among the most distinguished proponents of a somewhat similar neutrality thesis regarding speech in general is Yale law professor Owen Fiss. "The ideal of neutrality in the speech context," he writes,

> not only requires that the state refrain from choosing among viewpoints, but also that it not structure public debate in such a way as to favor one viewpoint over another. The state must act as a high-minded parliamentarian, making certain that all viewpoints are fully and fairly heard.[19]

What is anathema, according to this view, is the state's active tilting on behalf of a particular vision of how best to live one's life, including its political dimensions. Those decisions are to be left up to autonomous citizens, who make up their minds independent of the presumptively baleful influence of the state.

But Fiss offers an interesting twist on the neutrality argument, for he would in fact allow the state to take account of specifically unorthodox points of view that are in danger of being swamped in public conversation by the flood of conventional wisdom. Fiss's First Amendment is rooted in a vision of "collective self-determination" that requires a rich and full public debate once famously described by Justice Brennan, Fiss's hero, as "uninhibited, robust, and wide-open." This seemingly entails that the state can never inhibit or narrow the scope of public debate. Indeed, writing of public funding of the arts, Fiss condemns the failure to fund controversial projects on the ground that this in effect "impoverish[es] public debate" by "reinforc[ing] the prevailing orthodoxy. . . ." Fiss's ideal neutral state in fact turns out to be a self-conscious antagonist of congealed conventional wisdom.

There is a rich and nuanced literature that criticizes this view. I want to treat only the facet of the issue that is especially relevant to this book. I have been asking which people or what ideas are worthy of state honor, leaving quite unexamined an important prior question: Can the state properly honor anyone, or celebrate any particular views, at all? Although this question might well strike many readers as more than a bit odd, it follows quite easily from such views as the neutrality thesis. One might well ask why its devotees do not find highly problematic such standard practices as erecting monuments, naming streets, airports, and other public places after presumptive heroes, or issuing stamps commemorating "great Americans."

This image of the state as either benignly neutral or, perhaps even more remarkably, supportive of unorthodox ideas, is quite naive, not least because it almost wholly fails to pay adequate attention to the fact that the state is often an active participant in the intellectual marketplace. The easiest examples, of course, involve presidents giving major policy addresses or teachers using state-mandated textbooks within the public school system. Both regularly articulate, clothed in the full symbolic and actual authority of the state, highly contestable—and completely unneutral—views on important political and cultural matters. The danger facing those who disagree with the state's views comes, most often, not from any plausible fear of classic censorship—i.e., overt punishment for offering views repugnant to state authorities—but, rather, from being drowned out of the marketplace by the often superior re-

sources of the state.

The state may benefit from having more economic resources to articulate its position than do its opponents. But one should be aware that not the least valuable of the resources available to the state is its ability to legitimate certain arguments merely by virtue of being the state. From this perspective, the main threat posed by the state is that it will become an overweening tutor of the public, molding a distinct consciousness, and subtly (or not so subtly) delegitimizing others who would wish to play a similarly tutelary role. This, among other things, is the reason why the New Orleans City Council tried to establish and articulate, for educational purposes, an official view of the Liberty Monument quite at odds with the one carved on the monument's sides.

What might be termed "cultural regulation" occurs not only—indeed, increasingly rarely, in the United States—through the negative acts of overt silencing by threat of punishment to those with given views; more often, in the modern state, it occurs through the affirmative acts of the state as when it speaks on behalf of the people, or community, in whose name the state commonly claims to rule. Anyone influenced even slightly by Michel Foucault will recognize that the state devotes much of its resources to defining what is "regular" or, ultimately, "normal," within a given political-cultural order. Formally interdictive norms of the "thou shalt not" variety are only one method—and not necessarily the most important one—by which a state regulates and helps to manufacture what will count, in the language of our day, as politically correct. In any event, many citizens, from a variety of political perspectives, increasingly express their fear of a state that so dominates the marketplace that alternative conceptions of the public good will find themselves not so much silenced—at least in the specific sense of becoming legally unsayable— as relegated to the margins of the social order because of the lack of resources possessed by those who wish to speak contrary to the state's preferred vision. Those fearful of a tutelary state may even suggest that state speech itself on occasion be subject to censorship, though, from a traditional liberal perspective, it sounds wilfully paradoxical to speak of the state as the object of censorship rather than the agency that (usually illegitimately) censors others.

To be sure, one should note that the dominance of the state is at bottom an empirical question rather than a conceptual given. A pervasive theme of our time, after all, is the de facto dissolution of the state as a hegemonic entity that can exercise control over anything very important, whether it be economic development or general cultural developments. One need only point to the desperate attempts of states to control the Internet. The state does, of course, continue to enjoy the ability to inflict death and destruction on large numbers of people, though even here we saw that the possession of nuclear weapons did not enable the Soviet Union to survive or Israel successfully to supress the Palestinian *intifada*. Though it is undoubtedly premature to speak of the "withering away of the state," it seems clear that one must recognize an institutional pluralization in which the state is only one of many competitors for whatever goods — power, legitimacy, economic resources — are being sought. One might acknowledge all of this while still wondering how the empirically waning power of the state, assuming that this is occurring, affects the conceptual critique of the unneutral state.

The central question, then, is whether the United States Constitution can legitimately be read as limiting the power of either the national or state government to state certain views. The easiest justification of an affirmative answer, as already suggested, lies in the First Amendment's ban on the establishment of religion and the "no endorsement" interpretation given it by a majority of the current Supreme Court. Thus there is wide, even if not unanimous, agreement that Congress could not constitutionally legislate the addition of "In Christ Is Our Redemption" to the flag or the coinage. Nor is it clear that a city being founded today could choose to name itself Corpus Christi or, for that matter, St. Paul, insofar as such naming could plausibly be viewed as a way to regulate basic aspects of our culture in favor of religion. Indeed, apropos the principal topic of this book, it seems clear that public bodies could not place crosses in public space, and I would find problematic building a monument, say, to Billy Graham insofar as his life's mission has been Christian evangelism. (I should note, though, that there is indeed a Billy Graham Parkway in Charlotte, North Carolina.) Although there are many monuments now to Martin Luther King Jr., I would justify them, in contrast to the hypothetical monument to Graham, on the basis of King's passionate devotion to American society. Admittedly, it is misleading to separate King's religious identity from his public persona. Still, the point is that there was in King (or in Mother Teresa or the late Joseph Cardinal Bernadin of Chicago) a distinctly public dimension that complemented what might be termed their religious selves, and it is that public dimension that the state must emphasize even though other institutions, such as the Catholic Church, might well choose to focus on their religious identities.

In the age of the activist state, governmental speech is a pervasive method of regulation, and we have yet to achieve any satisfying way of coming to terms with it. It has become a cliché of contemporary social theory that political communities are the products of imagination, constructed by a variety of sociocultural projects, many of which are sponsored by the state. The setting for creation of these political communities is, almost always, what the detached social scientist would readily describe as a fractionated social order—sometimes multicultural or multinational, sometimes only divided along class or ideological grounds—whose centrifugal pressures may well put any notion of a unified polity under great stress. One might suggest, therefore, that a central task of the state is, by apt speech, to draw together an otherwise fractured community and thus, as promised by our own national motto, create *e pluribus unum.*

This is, of course, one rationale for a highly self-conscious program of civic education, where the metaphor of the state as tutor becomes most clearly instantiated. Benjamin Rush, one of our own founders, referred to the task facing the American republic as the creation, through education, of "republican machines," which means, among other things, that a youngster should "learn that he does not belong to himself, but that he is public property. Let him be taught to love his family, but let him be taught, at the same time, that he must forsake and even forget them, when the welfare of his country requires it." Less extreme, but nonetheless in the same spirit, is the statement of Abraham Lincoln that every child receive "at least a moderate education, and [be] thereby enabled to read the histories of his own and other countries, by which he may duly appreciate the value of free institutions."

The most obvious forum for such education is the public school, and ever-more-bitter debates course through our society as to state regulation of public education and its ostensible censorship of unpopular views. Fundamentalist Christians tend to focus on such issues as the failure to engage in respectful presentation of the claims of creation science, while some of those who speak in the name of contemporary multiculturalists angrily scrutinize public school textbooks to determine if enough space was devoted, with the proper attitude, to their favorite groups. What no one can seriously doubt, though, is that the state, when deciding upon curricula, is necessarily choosing one particular view (or set of views) among many others that might be suggested and, at least in other states, adopted.

If formal schooling is the most obvious example of self-conscious civic education designed to create, or at least to maintain, a privileged notion of community identity, the relevance of public monuments and the like should by now also be clear. As Will Kymlicka writes in his recent book *Multicultural Citizenship*, "Governmental decisions on languages . . . , public holidays, and state symbols unavoidably involve recognizing, accommodating, and supporting the needs and identities of particular ethnic and national groups. The state unavoidably promotes certain cultural identities, and thereby disadvantages others." Another political theorist, Michael Walzer, writing in *On Toleration*, suggests that even the most tolerant state is likely to have only one civil religion that necessarily disadvantages alternative understandings. "Civil religion," writes Walzer, "consists of the full set of political doctrines, historical narratives, exemplary figures, celebratory occasions, and memorial rituals through which the state impresses itself on the minds of its members. . . . How can there be more than one such set for each state?" Few questions are more important, especially in the age of the truly multicultural state.

Fiss's vision of the neutral, parliamentarian state can scarcely survive this much more vigorous vision of the state as inevitably privileging certain understandings of the community. Given his emphasis on the state's role in "bringing before the public viewpoints and options that otherwise might be slighted or ignored," perhaps he would allow the naming of a street after, say, Louis Farrakhan, but, surely, it would be far more problematic to reinforce a preexisting public orthodoxy by building yet another statue of, or naming one more street after, Martin Luther King Jr. (Indeed, perhaps one should suggest building a statue of one of King's savage opponents, such as Birmingham Police Commissioner "Bull" Connor.) If one rightfully finds these suggestions bizarre, then perhaps this suggests the limits of "neutrality" as a comprehensive approach to the role of the state in structuring the social consciousness. Surely Kymlicka and Walzer are correct in arguing the near impossibility of imagining a state that does not try to structure some set of privileged, constitutive, understandings of the society it purports to represent. And this is true, perhaps even especially true, of a liberal state whose law tolerates direct attacks on those understandings by ordinary citizens.

It simply cannot plausibly be argued that a conscientious constitutional interpreter, whether judge or legislator, must rigorously deny the state the right to speak unneutrally insofar as it selects out some small fraction of humanity as heroes whose lives (and life choices) should be emulated by us today. Public monuments that designate communal heroes or sacred communal events throughout time have been ways by which regimes of all stripes take on a material form and attempt to manufacture a popular consciousness conducive to their survival. Recall Kirk Savage's comment that public namings, whether of monumental heroes or simple street sites, "represent a kind of collective recognition—in short, legitimacy—for the memory deposited there." Legitimacy is a classic scarce resource; no social order bestows it promiscuously (even though many bestow it unwisely).

Should one look for support from the United States Supreme Court, one finds the fascinating 1896 case of *United States v. Gettysburg Electric Co.*, which involved the condemnation of electric company land in order to build a variety of monuments to the Battle of Gettysburg. The question was whether using the land as a venue for monuments constitutes a "public use" that the Fifth Amendment seemingly requires as a prerequisite to condemnation of private property by the state. Writing for a unanimous Supreme Court, Justice Rufus Peckham, one of the most stalwart devotees of property rights ever to serve on the Court, had no difficulty agreeing that the electric company could be forced to turn over its property to the state (after receiving "just compensation," of course). The monuments to be erected were, according to the Court, "so closely connected with the welfare of the republic itself as to be within the powers granted Congress by the Constitution for the purpose of protecting and preserving the whole country." And why is this the case?

The answer is that monuments will provide "proper recognition of the great things that were done there on those momentous days. By this use the government manifests for the benefit of all its citizens the value put upon the services and exertions of the citizen soldiers of that period." And this is no idle obeisance to the past. The efforts of these citizen soldiers to preserve the republic "is forcibly impressed upon every one who looks over the field." Congress's willingness to expend public funds and construct the monuments, said Peckham,

> touches the heart, and comes home to the imagination of every citizen, and greatly tends to enhance his love and respect for those institutions for which these heroic sacrifices were made. The greater the love of the citizen for the institutions of his country the greater is the dependence properly to be placed upon him for their de-

fense in time of necessity, and it is to such men
that the country must look for its safety.

There is, to put it mildly, nothing neutral about this
public use, anymore than there was in the exhortation by
Senator Moyhnihan that the Pennsylvania Avenue Development Commission encourage buildings of "monumental quality" that would "provide visual testimony to the
dignity, enterprise, and vigor of the federal government."
Nor is neutrality what comes to mind when reading the
congressional statute establishing the National Air and
Space Museum and mandating what kind of exhibits it
should contain: "The valor and sacrificial service of the
men and women of the Armed Forces shall be portrayed
as an inspiration to the present and future generation of
America." Not surprisingly, this statute was cited by some
of those who opposed the very controversial exhibit concerning the Enola Gay and the bombing of Hiroshima;
they argued that, by questioning the necessity or morality
of using the atomic bomb, the museum would necessarily
be violating its duty to present an inspirational picture of
the use of air and space technology by the United States.
Finally, it is worth mentioning that "public," in this
context, refers primarily to the placement and ideological function of the objects in question. Quite often, of
course, as in the *Gettysburg* case, they will be funded by
the taxpayers, and be "public" in that very fundamental

sense as well. Yet it is not at all unusual for private individuals or groups to finance monuments while seeking, through their display in a particular setting, the state's special imprimatur for the message contained within the monument. Michele H. Bogart notes, for example, that New York's Central Park quickly became a target of various groups, "especially those representing European immigrants," who "saw gifts of statues for Central Park as an appropriate way to beautify their city and to legitimate their heritage as well as their newfound status as Americans."[20] It is this imprimatur, however funded, that makes the state an active participant in the molding of the general culture. As a practical matter, then, a legal attack on memorials to the Confederate dead or the flying of the Confederate battle flag over state capitols must surely rest on something other than the purported duty of the state to maintain neutrality on basic political issues (other than the virtue of robust debate itself).

The Fourteenth Amendment and the
suppression of racist speech

If neutrality as such is unavailing, then perhaps the answer lies in a vigorous, and decidedly unneutral, reading of the Fourteenth Amendment in regard to its role in overcoming America's legacy of racial hierarchy and subordination. James Forman Jr. offers such a reading in arguing that Alabama was violating the Constitution in flying the Confederate flag on its state capitol.[21] Forman analyzes a 1990 case, *NAACP v. Hunt*,[22] which involved a challenge to the flying of the Confederate flag atop the Alabama capitol in Montgomery, where it flew immediately below the U.S. and Alabama state flags. The flag was first placed there in 1961, during a commemoration of the centennial of the Civil War. Apparently it was taken down shortly thereafter, for the opinion informs us that "the flag was raised again on the morning of April 25, 1963, the day that United States Attorney General Robert F. Kennedy travelled to Montgomery to discuss with then-Governor George Wallace the governor's announced intention to block the admission of the first black students to the University of Alabama." It flew for almost thirty years, until Governor Jim Folsom ordered its removal. Interestingly enough, Folsom apparently ordered that the Confederate battle flag continue to be flown across the street from the capitol at the First White House of the Confederacy, which presumably serves as a museum rather than the instantiation of contemporary Alabama. So it was not truly removed from public view even though it lost the special imprimatur provided by its place above the capitol dome.

Litigation challenging the flag had been undertaken as far back as 1975, and a second suit was filed in 1988. The NAACP's effort to use the Constitution to force Alabama to lower the Confederate flag gained no judicial support. "It is unfortunate," said the Eleventh Circuit Court of Appeals, "that the State of Alabama chooses to utilize its property in a manner that offends a large proportion of its population, but that is a political matter which is not within our province to decide." Apparently, appeal lies with the voting box and not the judiciary. It is worth noting that the author of this opinion was Judge Frank Johnson, who as a district judge in Alabama was often a lonely beacon of commitment to civil rights. From the perspective of most white Alabamans, Judge Johnson was always ready to invalidate majority decisions whenever they conflicted with constitutional values of racial equality. His refusal to

find that such values required lowering the Confederate flag, even as he freely admitted that many Alabamans were offended by its display over the capitol, thus has a special resonance.

James Forman disagrees with the court: He argues that "removing the Confederate flag is constitutionally required." For him there is nothing innocent about the flag as a political symbol. It signifies an entire system of racial oppression:

> The flag's force as a symbol stems from its history. The flag was initially designed as a rallying symbol for Confederate troops heading into battle. The rebels were fighting for territory, for economic control, and—it goes without saying —for slavery. . . . The Confederate flag glorifies and memorializes this brutal regime [of chattel slavery].
>
> But the Confederate flag symbolizes more

than the Civil War and the slavery era. It also stands for a history of resistance to change in the twentieth century. . . . The flag has been adopted knowingly and consciously by government officials seeking to assert their commitment to black subordination.

Thus, when a state government chooses to fly the flag above its capitol's dome, it "sends a message . . . glorif[ying] and memorializ[ing] slavery, Jim Crow, and subsequent resistance to change." Not only does the Confederate flag not serve as a symbol of a united nation, as does, one may hope, the American flag; it more properly is a marker for a *herrenvolk* democracy in which the members of one specific nation, Southern whites, exercised hegemony over another, Southern African Americans. Forman quotes a telling comment by Yale law professor Akhil Reed Amar: "Confederate symbols—flags, monuments, and so on—all too easily exclude large numbers of citizens, most notably blacks." One need not be a Yankee law professor (or an African American) to have this view. Surely a similar perception underlies the remark of South Carolina's Governor Beasley that "any banner we choose to fly over the Capitol . . . should be one that everyone can claim as their own." His own, albeit unsuccessful, call for the lowering of the flag presumably concedes the unreasonableness of expecting all South Carolinians to claim the flag as their own.

These are, of course, general statements that would presumably refer to any and all displays of the flag. But key to Forman's analysis is the fact that the flag was ultimately given its place of honor atop the capitol as one aspect of Alabama's attempt to resist desegregation of its public institutions. Thus he quite plausibly reads the raising of the flag in 1963 as "part of [George Wallace's] continuing effort to maintain white supremacy" and, therefore, under standard readings of the Fourteenth Amendment, proscribable as part of a remedial system designed to overcome the legacy of unconstitutional oppression. To be sure, Alabama offers a contrary historical analysis, claiming that it flew the flag in order to promote tourism and to preserve "historical value," as well as to symbolize "accomplishment, development, and progress towards racial equality." However, we are surely entitled to take this with an especially large grain of salt, just as we would be disdainful of any explanation of South Carolina's decision to fly the flag in 1962 that failed to mention the politics of resisting the civil rights movement.

Given Alabama's lack of any affirmative protection by the First Amendment, Forman argues that Alabama must defend the "legitimate government function" served by flying a symbol of such oppression. "It will take a creative legal mind," he wryly suggests, "to explain the utility of flying Dixie." "Utility" is an odd word in this context, for of course one explanation of the flag's presence is simply the presumptive pleasure gained by the majority of the voting population from seeing the flag waving over the capitol. Certainly one theory of democratic governance is that government can legitimately honor the preferences of the majority, especially if that majority can plausibly deny that its pleasure is simply a function of the displeasure caused their fellow citizens who are African American.

Consider in this context the heart-felt comments of Willie Morris, the brilliant, Mississippi-born, former editor of *Harper's*, author of a wonderful memoir called *North Toward Home*, who in fact ended up returning to Mississippi:

> In modern-day America, there is too much fashionable tampering with authentic tradition. At the peril which such contentions evoke, I argue that this juggling with expressions of the past is reminiscent of the way the communists are eternally rewriting history, obliterating symbols with each new guard. Finally, one could make a strong case that *Dixie* and the flag and the names "ole Miss" and "Rebels," deriving from old suffering and apartness and the urge to remember, are expressions of a mutual communal heritage, white and black, springing from the very land itself and its awesome strengths and shortcomings. As a historian friend of mine once remarked, "There's nothing wrong with the Confederate flag. The Civil War was fought over more than slavery." [23]

The historian Shelby Foote, one of the stars of Ken Burns's documentary on the Civil War, agrees. Although he recognizes that the battle flag "causes pain and that it has been misused by 'yahoos,' " he nonetheless views it as "a symbol of gallantry and other good—and bad—things," carried into battle by soldiers "who believed they were fighting for a noble cause." His solution is apparently to educate the "yahoos" about the deeper meanings of the flag as it continues to fly over the South Carolina Capitol.[24] There can be no doubt that these two eminences speak for many of their less famous Southern neighbors.

It is at this point that the issues raised by contemporary postmodernism become so relevant: One of the issues hovering over this entire debate is the hermeneutics of culture and the presence of sufficient interpretive clarity to say with confidence that what theorists might refer to as the flag-as-signifier refers to a unique signified (i.e. the system of chattel slavery). One might well believe, however, that the meaning of the flag is overdetermined, that is, subject to varying (and conflicting) interpretation. It is not that just any meaning can be assigned the flag; one need not embrace theories of radical indeterminacy. Rather, there are simultaneously present at least two determinate meanings of the flag-as-symbol-of-slavery and the flag-as-symbol-of-Southern-culture (independent of slavery)-and-local-autonomy. The flag is simultaneously an effort to remember what many Americans honor as a cherished past and to forget or to otherwise gloss over what many other

Americans consider to be the single most important aspect of that past. One might imagine in this context a battering husband who invites the victim of his violence to "remember the good times," especially if it is the case that there were in fact good times that might well be worth remembering. How does anyone, let alone a culture, come to terms with the inevitably mixed meanings of the symbols around which we organize our lives?

Then-Yale professor of law (and native Texan) Charles Black unforgettably argued thirty-five years ago, when chiding some of his legal colleagues for their doubts as to the legitimacy of *Brown v. Board of Education,* that only the most obtuse could fail to read the meaning of segregated schools in the South as inextricably linked with the centuries-long practice of racial subordination and humiliation. Most of us, regardless of our theoretical commitments, have little trouble accepting Black's analysis of the realities of 1954, even if we might wish to argue that the meaning of racially separate facilities is more complex today—an obviously debatable proposition. The question, though, is how often we have such high confidence in our own readings of our multicultures. And even if we do have such self-confidence, we might still ask how much we want courts to supply legally privileged readings—backed up by the force of the state—of culturally contested icons. In some of her Establishment Clause opinions, Justice O'Connor refers to the viewpoint of the "reasonable observer" in regard to deciding whether a particular phenomenon—say a Christmas-season crèche surrounded by Santa Claus and reindeer—endorses religion. As her critics point out, what counts as a reasonable response is precisely the heart of the problem, and it is not clear that those in judicial office, almost invariably denizens of the political establishment, are the best people to evaluate the claims asserted by those who will often be from well outside that establishment.

Forman's argument depends on just such a privileging of one particular interpretation and on the authority of one particular institution to offer authoritative interpretations of cultural artifacts. It is hard to see how anyone who has been touched (some would say "infected") by one or another variety of postmodernist theory can be entirely comfortable endorsing Forman's argument. At the very least it requires dismissing arguments like Morris's and Foote's (or Betty Sue Flowers's similar argument seen earlier in regard to the Liberty Monument). For me, at least, Morris is a credible witness as to the possibility of a nonracist meaning of the flag, in large part because of the nature of his general political and social commitments. The same is also true of Professor Flowers. I confess, though, that I have no hesitation in dismissing similar arguments when made by such people as the egregious Oliver North, who defended flying the flag during his unsuccessful Virginia campaign for the United States Senate in 1994, or by the New Orleans attorney who defends the Liberty Place monument on the ground that the battle it commemorates "had nothing to do with race. It had every-thing to do with angry people trying to take their rightful government back from an ignorant and corrupt Adminis-tration." It is the insistence that the battle "had *nothing* to do with race" that brands the statement as racist.

As already suggested, an especially effective part of For-man's argument is his emphasis on the specific context of Alabama's 1963 decision to add the flag to its capi-tol dome—George Wallace's defiance of federally court-ordered desegregation. Forman might well have offered a similar analysis of the 1962 decision by the South Carolina legislature to place the flag atop its statehouse, or, indeed, of Georgia's 1956 redesign of its flag, in which one is confi-dent that the desire to send a political message dominated any aesthetic concerns about flag design or desire to build a more truly united Georgia community. For Forman, in-corporating the Confederate battle flag in the state flag is the equivalent of a decision by the Georgia legislature to add the words "white supremacy" or "keep blacks in their place" to the state seal that is also featured on the state banner. Would it be any more legitimate to add those words than to add the words "Jesus Saves"? If one agrees with the earlier argument that the First Amendment prohibits the latter, then it seems equally thinkable that an amendment associated with a "new birth of freedom" would prohibit the state from articulating on its flag a message of white hegemony and African American subordination. And if one can accept this latter premise, then it would seem easy enough to extend it to what some regard as a symbolic, if not literal, utterance of the same sentiment.

As a careful lawyer, Forman frames his analysis within current legal doctrine, which requires, among other things, that government be shown to have intended the discriminatory consequences of its acts. To quote a term used in many recent Supreme Court cases, to be adjudged in violation of the Constitution, government must be shown to have acted "because of, rather than in spite of," any negative consequences visited upon minority groups. But it is notoriously difficult to prove malevolent intent, for reasons similar to those that plague the problem of interpretation in general.

Still, I do not embrace a universal skepticism. In fact, Forman is grimly lucky to have what lawyers call good facts, at least in regard to Georgia, South Carolina, and Alabama. It is almost impossible to view those states, at least as of 1956 and 1963, as motivated by anything other than the desire to engage in "the annoyance or oppression of a particular class" that even the Supreme Court of *Plessy v. Ferguson* pronounced itself ready to restrain. But, in their own way, these facts are almost too good. And, even in regard to these facts, it is not entirely clear how much events in 1963 should control our responses to a significantly different Alabama in 1997, nor is it clear how an analysis based on this 1963 facts would apply to decisions made under different circumstances.

Consider, for example, two high schools, one outside

Chicago, the other outside Cleveland, Ohio. The Thornton (Illinois) Fractional High School was divided in 1958 into North and South high schools. "At the time," wrote a reporter for the *Chicago Tribune,* "when the school was entirely white, it seemed clever and historical to connect South High School with Rebels [the name of the athletic team] and a Confederate flag." Similarly, the Willoughby (Ohio) South High School, when established around 1960, chose to call its teams "the Rebels and the Confederate flag gradually became part of the school's athletic traditions." As it happens, both schools chose to take down the flag when African American (and other) students protested. Would Forman require such elimination even though the initial choice almost certainly betrays far more a dreadful ignorance about American history and political symbolism rather than any conscious desire to make a political statement? (Sometimes, though, ignorance is itself so shameful as to warrant a vigorous response: Imagine our reaction to a decision by students at a new Germantown, Pennsylvania, high school to name themselves the "Germantown Nazis" and to adopt as their symbol the swastika because it is distinctive.)

Imagine also a possible decision by the state of Texas to fly on its capitol grounds the five flags (besides the American flag) that have, at one point or another in its history, represented the political territory now called Texas. Those are the flags of France, Spain, Mexico, the Lone Star Republic, and the Confederate States of America. Indeed, at least one state office building has these flags etched on its walls. Would Forman argue that only the first four should be unfurled or that the Confederate flag should be sand-blasted away from state buildings on which it now appears? One hopes that the answer is no, but perhaps the reason is that the best way to read such a display is as a narrative featuring the displacement of alien and long-since-forgotten identities by the ultimate embrace of the Texan-as-loyal-American. The very placement of the Confederate Flag with the French one suggests the irrelevance of the former instead of the continuing presence of a strongly French strain in contemporary Texan values. The more the Confederate Flag is dehistoricized, as it were, the more an onlooker can legitimately wonder what it says about the contemporary entity that chooses to fly it.

Perhaps the most problematic aspect of any argument that concentrates on the unique malevolence of the Confederate flag comes from the fact that it is surely, and tragically, not the case that slavery was protected only within the Confederacy. Why single *its* flag out for unique opprobrium? It is all too clear that it might be politically useful to demonize the Confederate flag precisely in order to avoid coming to terms with the potential negativity of the American flag, presented by its own apologists as necessarily evocative of "one nation, indivisible, with liberty and justice for all." Veneration of the Stars and Stripes, including the Pledge of Allegiance, can easily be regarded as means by which the state attempts to impose a certain narrative whose function is to blind us to the extent that the nation symbolized by the flag most certainly has not achieved such universal liberty and justice even for its own citizenry. And this has been true, of course, even after the defeat of the sociopolitical order symbolized by the Confederate flag and the formal abolition in 1865 of slavery that had hitherto been protected by established legal institutions.

These issues are all present in a distinctly nonhypothetical episode in which a Virginia judge ordered the removal of the Confederate flag from a Stafford, Virginia, courthouse exhibit on Virginia history, which included all of the emblems, including the British Union Jack, that had flown in the town of Stafford since the seventeenth century. The county's only African American judge, complaining that it was "not a symbol for equal justice for all," described the county law library, where the exhibit appeared, as an improper venue for historical education. "This is not a museum. This is a courthouse." A circuit judge ordered the removal of the Confederate flags, at which time the historians who arranged the exhibit removed all flags save for the Virginia and U.S. flags. "If you're going to take [the Confederate flag] down, take them all down," a historian was quoted. "You have to tell the history, warts and all." This last statement seems to me clearly correct.

I think that I might have the same reactions to the flying of the swastika as part of a similar exhibit in a German city devoted to careful acknowledgment of all facets of its past. It would be bizarre to jump from the flag of the Weimar Republic to that of the postwar successor states of East and West Germany and deny the fact that there was a German state, with its own distinctive flag, between 1933–45. But it is hard to deny the power of Forman's arguments in regard to the specifics of the Alabama decision to fly the Confederate flag or the Georgia decision to redesign the state flag. Still, even there, my inclination is to agree with the *Hunt* court, though I certainly believe that a well-trained lawyer could accept Forman's analysis. Part of the reason for my own hesitation is my belief that, whatever the value of courts—and constitutions—in limiting tangible oppression, they are quite limited in their actual power when what is at stake is the politics of cultural meaning. I think it unwise, as a general matter, to encourage judicial intervention in circumstances where the consequences are unlikely genuinely to advance one's overall social or political agenda and, indeed, are likely to provoke an unfortunate backlash.

Return for a moment to the example of religion and the Establishment Clause. I happen to believe that the placement of "In God We Trust" on the coinage is unconstitutional governmental speech, and I confess a temptation to force a number of the states whose state mottoes include reference to God—consider only Arizona ("*Diat Deus*," God Enriches) and Ohio ("With God, all things are possible")—to find more secular mottoes. That being said, I do not really believe that courts should invalidate the coinage or require the finding of new mottoes. Not everything that is arguably unconstitutional should be enjoined by the judiciary. Judicial caution is especially merited when the challenged practices have become sedimented in historical memory and are simply accepted as a status quo. Judicial invalidation would be viewed as disruption of this status quo, in contrast, say, to the proper invalidation of an attempt to revise the coinage to read even "In Jehovah We Trust"—thus identifying a specific God. It would be the adherents of the change who would be viewed as the disrupters, and the courts would more easily be able to gain support for their intervention.

Not all status quos, obviously, deserve respect, as illustrated most easily by the pre-1954 status quo of segregated schools. Yet, invariably, a certain amount of prudence must necessarily determine what role courts play in resolving social disputes. To be frank, the costs to the nonreligious (or simply to constitutional purists) of having to handle the tainted coinage are not sufficiently high to justify the political costs of judicial intervention in circumstances that would very clearly generate a firestorm of protest and, potentially, lead to much greater political mobilization by those opposed to such a decision than by those who support it. Courts, like all political institutions, have invariably limited resources, and it is foolish for the courts to pick fights that they almost certainly cannot win, unless the very highest issues of political morality are being raised. Even if one believes that justice must be done or else the heavens fall, such dire behavior is presumably required only in cases of the most extreme injustice. Otherwise, only the utopian can believe that even the best legal regime can escape from tolerating one or another degree of milder injustice.

Lest this sound too purely prudential, I also invoke the ideas of Yale law professor Robert Burt, who emphasizes in his work the value of courts as initiators of conversations and the undesirability of the judiciary's foreclosing such conversations by a too-quick readiness to use their coercive powers to declare that one conversational partner must simply capitulate to the other. Force of law is often little better than force of arms in genuinely bringing about a political community in which people of radically different cultures and political views can live in truly mutual respect and equal citizenship. That being said, I must also recognize that I am not at all clear about what will bring about such respect in a self-consciously multicultural society like our own.

The *Hunt* court wisely chose not to invest its inevitably scarce political capital in a decision that would most likely have generated similar firestorms without either making the lives of Southern African Americans noticeably better off in tangible terms or truly generating the kind of political community built on the mutual respect and affection that a democracy needs. Forman might well remind us that we do not live by bread alone; Justice Holmes reminded us long ago, after all, that "we live by symbols," and foolish indeed is the person who underestimates their importance. Symbols are an important part of the cultural exchange system that, among other things, establishes relationships of hierarchy and domination. The result of a court's staying its hand may not be the initiation of conversation but, rather, the maintenance of an unacceptable status quo of domination and oppression. But one must still ask what it is that courts can best do and when they should stay their hand, and I remain inclined to believe that the judges were properly cautious in *Hunt*. I do not know the specific circumstances of the decision by an Alabama state judge to order the removal of the flag from the capitol under an 1895 state law. Suffice it to say that I find it far preferable that such a decision be made by a local judge applying Alabama's own law instead of a federal court invoking constitutional norms.

My caution concerning legal invalidation of the Confederate flag is heightened in regard to the monument for the war dead, which, if anything, presents even more wrenching semiotic issues than does the flag. Recall that its self-presentation had literally nothing to do with slavery and everything to do with basic American notions of self-determination by the constituent states of the union. To be sure, those notions have lost out over time to Marshallian conceptions of a single constituent entity called the people of the United States, with states playing no fundamental constitutive role. But does this mean that we should indeed consign these losing ideas to the dustbin of history, or might they be worth memorializing—and reflecting upon—as worthy alternatives to the road actually taken?

Consider also the date of the construction of the Texas monument: 1901. Michael Kammen writes that "the decades between 1870 and 1910 comprised the most notable period in all of American history for erecting monuments in honor of mighty warriors, groups of unsung heroes, and great deeds." The great period of monument building in the South was the first decade of the twentieth century, in part because it took so long to emerge from the poverty generated by the war. In addition to economic considerations, though, one can assume that by 1901 most survivors of the battles of 1861–65 were at least in their late fifties, if not older, and it would be strange indeed if they had no intimations of their own mortality. For many of these men, service in the war was presumably the most meaningful act of their lives.

One can well understand the desire to memorialize that service in a suitable monument, as well as the state's decision to accept the monument for display before what was then the relatively new capitol, where it would join other monuments, including one to the heroes of the Alamo. It is, I think, implausible to view the memorial as a latter-day attempt to vindicate slavery, even if one necessarily recognizes the intimate linkage between slavery and secession (and even if one wishes to condemn the monument builders for ignoring that linkage). Indeed, one might well interpret the almost desperate insistence to avoid slavery as implicitly recognizing its illegitimacy. After all, the text of the United States Constitution itself maintains a studied silence in regard to the nomenclature of slavery, and many have used this silence as evidence of the tacit opposition of the framers to the institution, whatever their pragmatic decision to collaborate in its maintenance.

But how important is the nomenclature? Imagine that the monument lacked the inscription set out above and said only "in memory of those who gave their lives fighting for the Confederacy." Would that be any more acceptable, or would one want to rule out all commemoration of Confederate soldiers? Does the Constitution indeed require the state to remain abjectly silent rather than honor the losers in the great American epic of 1861–65?

How one answers these questions would presumably have implications for that particular form of governmental action known as the public holiday. In Virginia, for example, Martin Luther King Jr.'s birthday is celebrated on the very same day as the equally official (Robert E.) Lee–(Stonewall) Jackson Day. In New Hampshire, the one state that has refused to establish Martin Luther King Jr. Day as a state holiday, some have proposed establishing a "Civil Rights Day," which has drawn opposition from those who view this as implicitly attacking the status of Dr. King.

An interesting variant can be found in Texas, which officially celebrates Confederate Heroes Day, which happens to occur during the same week as Martin Luther

King Jr.'s birthday, also celebrated as an official holiday in Texas. On King's birthday all state offices are closed, whereas on Confederate Heroes Day state offices remain open with skeleton crews and other employees who receive their supervisor's permission to come in and work. Many people, therefore, can, in effect, refuse to honor the Confederate heroes. But consider those who do not receive authorization to come in and work; they are forced to take a vacation day on behalf of the Confederates. Some would argue, though, that even those who do not in fact honor Dr. King are equally coerced, as is even more clearly the case with non-Christians who are forced to observe Christmas but who must take leave on non-Christian holidays out of their scarce allotment of personal vacation time. Ought the Constitution be read to control the declaration of such holidays and the public subsidy, through vacations, of celebrants? Under some circumstances, I would certainly say yes in regard to religious holidays. Christmas is, like the words "In God We Trust" on the coinage, a fait accompli that ought not be disturbed. But I enthusiastically support those courts that have struck down attempts by states to mandate Good Friday as an official holiday. Still, for many of the reasons set out earlier, I am dubious about extending such analysis to what might be termed "civil religious" holidays, including Confederate Heroes Day.

Beyond law: What does political decency require?

It should be obvious that legal analysis is only one way to approach the subject. That courts ought not strike down some practice does not in the least suggest that the practice is in fact commendable and ought not be changed, voluntarily, by decent people. And ordinary individuals, whether by writing letters to the editor or marching in demonstrations, might well encourage those in power to mend their ways. So, more important in many ways than the question of what courts ought to do, or even of what the Constitution, properly interpreted, is best understood to mean, is what we as ordinary citizens should do when claims such as Forman's are laid before us. He concludes his article with a heartrending reminiscence of his schooldays as a senior at the Franklin Delano Roosevelt High School in Atlanta and the discomfort, physical as well as emotional, caused by

> the incongruity of having black children, in a largely black city, watch a black man raise the symbol of the Confederacy for us all to honor. I tell myself to laugh, hoping that this will keep me from crying. But I cannot laugh, and I dare not cry, so I close my eyes and try to forget. If I could just forget. . . .[O]vercoming the flag has taken a piece of me—a piece that I will not easily recover.

Decent people should, I think, be repelled by a political system that leads to such consequences. Thus, in regard to the specific example of the Confederate flag, I think the answer is easy. Although I would, as a matter of civil liberties, defend the right of a private individual to wave the flag, and, as already noted, I would not have the courts prohibit a state from flying the flag, that does not in the least entail my support of any such behavior. The Confederate flag should be lowered from the state flagpoles on which it now flies. The governors of Georgia and South Carolina merit our applause for their attempts, even if so far fruitless, to wean their states from their addiction to the Confederate battle flag. In regard to the former, though, one might still wonder if it is adequate merely to adopt Governor Miller's suggestion, which is to change the design of the Georgia flag by returning to the 1905 flag, which was itself based on the official Confederate flag. After all, one could instead return to the 1799 flag, which featured the state seal, depicting wisdom, justice, and moderation, standing on a blue background representing loyalty.

Even if one can believe that the Confederate flag symbolizes something other than the brutal regime of chattel slavery, it seems insensitive, to put it mildly, for a state to persist in adopting as its official emblem something that so easily, and legitimately, can be given a thoroughly negative meaning. Still, even in regard to the flag, I would support its display in the "flags over Texas" exhibit hypothesized earlier or, for example, over some historic building that is strongly associated with the Confederacy or, even more strongly, within a cemetery for Confederate soldiers. It is also clear, I think, that the flag could be displayed within a museum setting. Indeed, the chair of the Alabama House of Representatives Black Caucus did not oppose the flag's flying over the Confederate White House across the street from the Capitol. "We have maintained all along," said Representative George Perdue, that "the Confederate battle flag should be relegated to some kind of historical display or museum." Perhaps the Confederate flag should be put in its place, but I cannot believe that it has no place in any conceivable public setting. To say that the state cannot speak strongly through the medium of the flag does not mean that the state must on all occasions erase it from its lexicon.

Monuments present altogether more difficult issues. For example, Dr. Clifton Johnson, director of the Amistad Research Center in New Orleans, one of the largest archival centers for research in African American history in the United States, defends preserving the Liberty Place monument on the ground that "racism is part of our history." The monument, he says, is a symbol of "racism's shame" and a reminder, especially to youngsters "of the courage of the whole civil rights movement." Similar analyses could presumably be offered of statues to Jefferson Davis, even though it is obvious that partisans of such statues would resent bitterly the "defense," if that is the proper word, offered by Dr. Johnson.

I conclude by offering a detailed menu of possibilities in regard to the Austin monument to the Confederate dead:

1. Leave it precisely as it is at present, doing nothing at all.

2. Erect, by the monument, a sign saying something to the effect of "The State of Texas takes no position on the views expressed on this monument."

3. Erect, by the monument, a sign saying something to the effect of "The views expressed on this monument do not represent the views of the State of Texas."

4. Erect, by the monument, a sign saying something to the effect of "These views were once held by many people, but we now know that this is a false view of the United States Constitution, and Texas in fact committed constitutional treason in attempting to secede," or, "Although these views represent a plausible constitutional theory, it is essential to recognize that what precipitated secession was the desire to maintain an immoral regime of racially-based chattel slavery. The failure of the white South to recognize the claim to equality and self-determination of black slaves thus invalidates the appeal to the principles of the Declaration of Independence that might, in another context, have justified secession and defense against Union efforts to prevent it."

5. Erect an adjoining monument to the Union dead, with (or without) some suitable Lincolnian statement about the inadmissability of secession and the necessity to preserve the Union.

6. Erect additional monuments, among which the following are possible:

a) A monument to those enslaved by Texans and other denizens of the Confederacy. This would, obviously, be similar to the *Mahnmale* in Germany.

b) A monument to those blacks who in fact fought for the Confederacy. This was actually suggested by one Virginian in regard to a debate that recently raged in Richmond about the meaning of Monument Avenue. The *Richmond Times-Dispatch* responded, "Well, why not dedicate a memorial somewhere to African-Americans who fought bravely for both sides?" This would, inevitably, be a monument to Unionist soldiers, insofar as "200,000 African-Americans, most of them freed slaves, fought in the Union Army." In fact, notes Columbia historian Eric Foner, many thousands of Mississippians fought for the Union. It's simply that most of us do not identify anyone nonwhite, especially those who had been held in slavery, as "Mississippians." Surely there were black Texans who fought for the Union who might be honored.

c) A monument to some appropriate African American. Potential candidates are legion. In Detroit, for example, one can find the deliciously mixed-meaning sculpture of a large fist, a memorial to the great boxer—and, in the language of my youth, "credit to his race"—Joe Louis. More recently a successful campaign was waged in Richmond, Virginia, led by former Governor Douglas Wilder, the first African American governor of Virginia, to raise funds to cast and place a twenty-four-foot statue of the late Arthur Ashe, who was originally from that city. What is most interesting, from the perspective of this essay, is the debate on precisely where to place the statue.

Governor Wilder, for example, felt that "it needs to be on Monument Avenue. It will send a transcending message." A columnist for the *Richmond Times-Dispatch* agreed:

> The avenue is an undeniable source of pride among many city and state residents. But the bronze Confederates who sit astride their steeds produce no small amount of ambivalence among the state's African-Americans. . . . Monument is the city's showcase boulevard. Let's make it a place where blacks and whites can share a sense of pride, in a spirit of reconcilation.

Perhaps the admirable spirit of reconciliation underlying this suggestion would have been even better manifested had the author recognized that ambivalence (at best) about the bronze Confederates might well be felt by many non-African Americans as well, a response that seems unthinkable to the editorialist. Would only Jews be upset by a German statue honoring the SS?

However, in an editorial, the *Richmond Times-Dispatch* disagreed with its own columnist: though warmly supporting the monument, it differed in regard to the site:

Enshrining the tennis star among Confederate War heroes on Monument Avenue . . . would strip Ashe's memory of context and deprive it of meaning. Further, many of those pressing for that site admit their chief motivation is to settle a racial score. Ashe deserves better than to be used as a political pawn by those who refract all perceptions through the prism of race.

If Ashe is to be honored for who he was and what he accomplished, then [a local park that includes tennis courts] makes a fitting site. What could offer more poetic justice than enshrining there a man once barred by segregation laws from playing on its courts?

Some analysts have suggested, incidentally, that Ashe himself, who apparently disliked being made use of as a racial or political symbol, might well have preferred the placement of his statue in the park rather than have it so obviously used to make a statement by being put on Monument Avenue. This raises additional questions of how people become appropriated by their culture for use as symbols independent of any of their own wishes. However, it appears that the Ashe family agreed to the Monument Avenue placement, though, of course, this may only be evidence for the proposition that Ashe would not have been actively opposed to that placement.

Interestingly enough, someone suggested that the better

addition to Monument Avenue would be a memorial to one of "the 200,000 men of African descent who fought for freedom and the Union in our nation's bloodiest conflict — men like Richmond-born Powhatan Beaty," a first sergeant who was awarded the Congressional Medal of Honor for his courage in the battle of New Market Heights, where he led a charge on entrenched Confederates despite his severe injuries. Similarly, Professor Foner, one of our most distinguished students of mid-nineteenth-century America, has urged that Virginia consider raising a statue to "Gabriel, who in 1800 plotted to liberate Virginia's slaves. . . . His followers planned to carry a banner bearing a slogan borrowed from Patrick Henry: 'Death or Liberty.' " Whether or not with tongue in cheek, Foner writes that "Gabriel epitomizes the heritage of freedom that Virginia claims." One may well be skeptical that either of these proposed monuments would have gained more genuine support than the one to Arthur Ashe. No such support would have been received, for example, from Samuel Francis, who, in a column entitled "The Second Civil War Comes to Richmond," writes that the purpose of Monument Avenue

> is explicitly to honor Virginians who led the Confederacy, and whatever the future of the state, the region or the nation, the Confederacy remains a real and central part of their real past. . . . If Virginians are going to preserve their real past and the real culture the past in-

forms, they'll have to show at least as much solidarity in its defense as the Afro-racists [sic] do for their cause. If they don't or won't, maybe the Confederate statues ought to take a hike to some other place where their heritage still means something.

Perhaps Francis would have endorsed the revival of a bill actually passed by the United States Senate in 1923 directing acceptance of a monument to be given by the Jefferson Davis Chapter No. 1650 of the United Daughters of the Confederacy "in memory of the faithful colored mammies of the South." (For whatever reason, the bill never got out of committee in the House of Representatives.)

In any event, the Richmond Planning Commission settled the matter on June 19, 1995, when it agreed to place the monument on Monument Avenue, though it subsequently took an extended meeting of the Richmond City Council to ratify the decision. As a writer for the *Richmond Times-Dispatch* put it, "Arthur Ashe's statue will penetrate the Confederacy's second line of defense after all." The penetration was successfully achieved in 1997, when the statue was indeed placed on Monument Avenue.

As for contemporary Texas, I have no doubt that it would be easy to gather support for placing on the Capitol lawn a statue of former Representative Barbara Jordan, the first African American to be elected to Congress from Texas and, thereafter, a powerful voice in American poli-

*Arthur Ashe on Monument Avenue, Richmond, Virginia
(Photograph by John Paul Jones).*

tics. Indeed, the Austin City Council recently voted to name its new municipal airport (which will replace the Bergstrom Air Force base) after her, though this decision drew an angry letter from someone who objected to the erasure from Austin's public memory of Bergstrom, an Austinite who fought heroically in World War I. (Similar objections were raised, incidentally, to the renaming of the University of Texas's Memorial Stadium to the Darryl Royall-Memorial Stadium, in honor of Texas's most successful football coach. Although Royall is in fact still alive, critics of the name change noted that almost no one will continue to commemorate the veterans intended to be honored by the original name.) Assuming that Texas would like to build a statue honoring Jordan, one can still wonder where, precisely, it should go. Should it be placed in explicit juxtaposition to the edifice to the Confederate war dead or should it receive an entirely separate (and equal?) setting somewhere else on the expanse of grass surrounding the Capitol?

7. Remove the monument to the museum of Texas history, where it would be placed in some suitable context involving Texas history between 1865–1901. An American precedent of sorts for such a move involves the statue representing the Fort Dearborn massacre in Chicago, which featured a presumably savage Indian about to plunge his tomahawk into the breast of the white maiden. The statue was taken off the lawn and placed within the walls of the Chicago Historical Society when a new entrance area was added in the late 1960s. Interestingly enough, one person recalls visiting the society in 1973 or 1974 and discovering "a basket of fruit and vegetables at the base of the statue, an 'offering,' a Scotch-taped sign read, 'of peace and love from the native American community which has been insulted and neglected by the Chicago Historical Society since its beginning.'" This only reinforces the fact that "museumization" will scarcely resolve the issues of multiple interpretations and the social cleavages underlying them.

8. Sandblast the presumptively problematic narrative of the war off the monument and either leave that side blank or replace it with some more acceptable statement, as was

done by New Orleans in regard to the Liberty Place Monument.

9. Destroy the monument.

It is probably easiest to begin with the last possibility, for I find it only slightly less difficult to support destruction of the monument than to imagine an actual decision by the State of Texas to do so. At the very least, advocacy of its destruction involves embracing the politics of *kulturkampf*—cultural warfare—to the ultimate degree.

Hundreds of thousands of Southerners lost their lives in the misguided attempt at secession and maintenance of slavery. Is it really impossible to convey a certain amount of public honor to those dead, the overwhelming majority of them decidedly ordinary people who responded to primordial notions of loyalty and service on behalf of what they viewed as their country? If the obnoxiousness of the Lost Cause prevents any public memorialization, then why do many of us find so immensely moving the Vietnam War Memorial in Washington even if (or perhaps especially if) we believe, as I continue to do, that that war was little (if any) more defensible than that fought by the Confederacy? Perhaps one would emphasize that the Vietnam Memorial, very importantly, does not include any writing specifying the "correct" political message of the black granite and the fifty thousand names. But this can't be the whole truth either, even if we ignore the fact that a more conventional and heroic statue was added at the site at the insistence of veterans groups who found Maya Lin's great memorial too unheroic. I would object to memorializing the SS at Bitburg even if the only message contained on a monument was "Rest in Peace." I wish to offer no respect at all to these soldiers, and I most certainly do not hope that they are resting in peace, whatever that might mean. What I view as key, though, is that SS members were not ordinary citizen-soldiers like those commemorated on the Vietnam Memorial (or the Confederate monuments).

The other alternatives that I have offered Texas are obviously more complex, even though, practically speaking, one doubts that Texas would adopt any of them other than the first, which is to do nothing at all. The seventh alternative represents the full historicization linked with the museum itself as a cultural phenomenon. But historicization is itself obviously a complex phenomenon, for one always wonders whether the message is that "this was once, but can—ought—never be again" or, instead "this was once and can, with imaginative effort and physical courage, be repeated in our own lifetime." I suspect that museum curators themselves, especially if the museums themselves are public entities, would be faced with genuinely difficult choices concerning the presentation of the material.

One certainly could take no encouragement from the fiasco in the spring of 1995 concerning the proposed exhibit at the Smithsonian Institution's National Air and Space Museum of the Enola Gay, the plane from which the first atomic bomb was dropped on Hiroshima on August 6, 1945. Outraged (and, in my opinion, outrageous) protest from veterans groups and others made it impossible to mount a professionally competent exhibition regarding the controversy surrounding the use of the bomb. The exhibition was canceled, and Dr. Martin Harwit, director of the museum, resigned. An editorial in the *Washington Post* noted that the "much-abridged version of the Enola Gay exhibit," consisting apparently of the bare fuselage of the plane, would be, in the words of the museum itself, "commemorative rather than interpretive," thus avoiding any confrontation with the issues of historical interpretation that doomed the original project. The editorial further describes officials of the Smithsonian, including its secretary, former Berkeley law professor Ira Michael Heyman, as conceding that "mixing 50-year commemorative anniversary ceremonies with hotly contested revisionist analysis is a bad idea generally." The *Post* gives no indication that it disagrees, which is dismaying in regard to the capacity of a society genuinely to confront its past, warts and all, rather than to settle for almost mindless celebration and the complacent maintenance of unexamined assumptions about the events in question.

Would building a monument to the Union dead, accompanied by Lincolnian denunciation of secession and slavery, suffice? Or does it simply create a semiotic jumble satisfying to enough political constituencies to bring civil peace in its wake? Civil peace is no small matter, and great political theory has been written in behalf of its centrality. So should Texas emulate Jefferson by proclaiming

"We are all Unionists, we are all Confederates"? Perhaps the correct answer to this question is an all-too-easy yes. Edward Linenthal, for example, has noted that what enabled Gettysburg to become a jointly shared vehicle for the reconciliation of North and South was a mutual glorification of martial courage, coupled with the subordination of any emphasis on the issue of slavery—and the quality of the freedom that followed 1865. This subordination, of course, underlay the Compromise of 1877 that reconciled Southern and Northern whites by ending Reconstruction and accepting the return of the South—and its millions of former slaves—to the rule of white Democrats. So perhaps more to the point is whether anyone disinclined to accept the Compromise and its devastating consequences for racial justice would offer such a proclamation. Linenthal indicates his own position by quoting Frederick Douglass's 1894 remark, "I am not indifferent to the claims of a generous forgetfulness, but whatever else I may forget, I shall never forget the difference between those who fought to save the Republic and those who fought to destroy it." One assumes that Douglass equates saving the Republic with overcoming slavery.

Several alternatives involve overt state speech, in which those who control the contemporary state apparatus comment on the views of their ancestors. One of the alternatives does involve Texas articulating an official view of the war that negates the monument's message. The problem with this alternative (again putting political practicality aside) is that, as suggested earlier, there is no very good reason to accept the view of "an indivisible Union of indestructible States"—articulated, appropriately enough, in a case called *Texas v. White*—as the undoubtedly correct view of the Constitution. I personally find the constitutional arguments on behalf of secession quite plausible, especially if one reads the Constitution in light of the Declaration of Independence's emphasis on the consent of the governed. What undercuts any support I might have for the Confederacy is not the Union metaphysics enunciated by Lincoln and endorsed in *White*, but rather the reality of chattel slavery. Rather than have Texas, in effect, apologize for attempting to secede, I would prefer that Texas, even while acknowledging the abstract plausibility of secessionist theory, address the fact that it was used to defend an indefensible way of life. This would, as a formal matter, leave the original 1903 monument untouched, still able to work its own power on an onlooker who ignores the sign or dismisses it as an egregious example of contemporary political correctness.

The second alternative, in which Texas simply disclaims adherence to the message without offering one of its own, is analogous to those seen in many airports in regard to solicitors engaging in their own constitutionally protected speech. But, of course, what makes airport disclaimers persuasive is precisely the fact that the speakers are private citizens exercising their own constitutional rights without any real cooperation from the state beyond recognition that they cannot be removed from public property. It is altogether plausible to believe that the administrators of O'Hare airport are indifferent, and quite possibly hostile, to the ideas that they are required to tolerate. But Texas is scarcely in that position, at least in regard to the monument. Even if it did not commission the statue, it nonetheless accepted it on behalf of the state. As of 1903, at least, one presumes that the message of the statue was altogether compatible with the views of dominant political elites. It is certainly crystal clear that there is no right to place on the grounds in front of the capitol any statuary one wishes, any more than one could claim that the presence of the Washington, Lincoln, and Vietnam Memorials on the national Mall in Washington would entitle one to construct, even without governmental funds, a monument, say, to the Native American victims of American aggression or to the Japanese victims of atomic warfare. Government does indeed speak when it offers sacred space even for privately commissioned entities like the new Holocaust Museum in Washington. One could not, therefore, credit a simple disclaimer of support by Texas, especially so long as Texas continues to include Confederate Heroes Day on its official calendar.

If forced to choose, I would opt for a set of monuments, of sufficient grandeur and placed in the heart of the Capitol grounds, commemorating different aspects of the African American experience. Given the reality of Texas history, this would include slavery and the exploitation and racial segregation that followed the demise of legal slavery, but I would be shocked if African Americans would want to reduce their history only to these realities, any more than I, as a Jew, accept reduction of Jewish history to victimization in the Holocaust. Thus a monument to Barbara Jordan, among others, should also be an important part of any such display. Though I would welcome the development of a consensus among Texans that would accept the move of the Confederate monument away from the capitol to a museum, I would certainly not do so in the absence of any such development.

Perhaps the most attractive idea comes from University of Colorado historian Patricia Nelson Limerick, writing in the *New York Times* about the controversy over adding to the Little Bighorn National Monument a $2 million memorial to American Indian dead as a complement to the memorial to the U.S. soldiers who died there.[25] The debate currently focuses on the issue of which particular interpretive perspective is to dominate. Limerick, however, "imagine[s] a different kind of memorial—one in which no point of view dominates," in which many monuments to all sorts of people would contend for recognition. "Would this add up to a coherent and clear historical lesson? Of course not. But the event itself was not the least bit coherent or clear." This leads to her most delicious suggestion, that the National Park Service "designate a nearby area as a Managed Contention Site," which "would provide an arena for presentations by today's partisans.

Physical violence would be prohibited, but heated verbal disagreements over history would be encouraged." There is something extraordinarily attractive about the idea of "managed contention sites," but only, of course, if we accept the proposition that there are legitimate debates to be held. Consider that within five days the *Times* published a letter to the editor complaining that Professor Limerick's desire that no single point of view dominate historical memorials leads to the possibility of "future proposals from revisionist historians on the construction of memorials to the Mexican dead at the Alamo and the Japanese at Iwo Jima." What is interesting about this jibe, of course, is the assumption that the very idea of such memorials (or, perhaps more accurately, "countermemorials") is self-evidently absurd, which is true only so long as the winners of those particular battles maintain their hegemony over historical memory. Having said this, though, I acknowledge my own discomfiture at the idea of using the legitimacy of disagreements over history as the excuse for offering a platform to those, for example, who deny the historical reality of the Holocaust or the malignity of chattel slavery. At that point, a due respect for the legitimacy of multiple perspectives, which I endorse, would indeed become the anything-goes kind of historical relativism that many of the critics of multiculturalism decry. So we return to the central dilemma sketched in this book.

Coda

We do indeed live by symbols, whether they are tangible pieces of colored cloth or marble depictions of those the culture wishes to honor, or the more intangible messages generated by days of commemmoration and celebration. To the extent that our world increasingly features either dramatic regime changes, as in Eastern Europe, or the self-conscious recognition of the multicultural status even of stable political states, it should not surprise us that these symbols have become, in the language of contemporary philosophy, "essentially contested," with significant political energy put into achieving one or another resolution of such contests. We must, of course, try to clarify our own responses to these symbols, but it is naive in the extreme to believe that we can achieve any genuine consensus as to their place in the public realm. That would require the existence of a singular public, whereas the reality of our society is its composition by various publics who are constituted at least in part by their relationship to conflicting symbologies. And, needless to say, all of these publics seek the particular validation that comes from their symbols occupying some place of respect within the general public realm. It is, therefore, no small matter whether these publics can indeed agree on some common civil rites and symbols or whether we are indeed doomed to an ever-more-fractionated discourse about the most basic use of public space and the construction of a public narrative (and, ultimately, a public psyche) that pays due heed to the complexities of the past that we share, with whatever unease.

While trying to think through the issues raised in this book, I found myself imagining a divorced couple—or, perhaps more accurately, two such couples. The first was torn asunder by the abusive practices of one of the spouses. In this instance, I assume that we would surely not criticize the victimized party not only for ending the marriage, but also for taking down pictures of her former spouse or, perhaps, taking advantage of contemporary technology that allows one simply to excise from a picture those people one does not wish to see. This could indeed be a most healthy step in "getting on with one's life," which in this instance might require the psychological eradication of the Other. Our understanding of, or even sympathy with, such acts would not, however, mean that we might not wish to cheer a second couple who, having decided on an amicable divorce upon the joint realization that their mutual growth lay elsewhere than in continuing bonds of matrimony, prove able to honor their past lives and to retain material representations—nongrandiose monuments—of those lives together within their now separate homes. Jack Balkin has suggested, though, that this evocation of a divorced couple is profoundly misleading, that the real point is not what they would do, but, rather, how their children (or, indeed, grandchildren) would respond. The one thing we know for sure is that all veterans of the great struggles of 1861–65, and all of the slaves whose lives were so affected by that struggle, are long since dead. We must decide to what extent we wish to acknowledge, or to repudiate, our symbolic ancestors. What do we do with otherwise cherished family pictures upon the discovery that one's ancestors were far more checkered, indeed perhaps even villainous, than the earlier, more comforting, family narrative had suggested?

One might hope that even the partisans of quite radical regime changes would nonetheless recognize that their now-supplanted predecessors were not without valuable qualities, perhaps worth honoring by maintaining existing public monuments or even by building some new ones. But such pacific and ideologically generous regime changes are almost certainly the exception rather than the rule (as may be the case with truly amicable divorces and children who escape unharmed from those divorces). As noted earlier, whatever the specialness of our relationship to the mother country of Great Britain, the United States has put up no monuments honoring even Benedict Arnold, let alone General Cornwallis. Far more ominous is Eric Foner's reminder that "participation in Reconstruction is enough to exclude even some prominent Confederates from the pantheon of Southern heroes. No monuments to [Confederate] Gen. James Longstreet grace Southern towns because he supported black rights after the Civil War."

Or consider the lowly commemorative stamp, issued by most countries as a quite inexpensive way to memorialize civil worthies. The British have never published a stamp commemorating Oliver Cromwell, nor have the French put any of their former kings on their postage. It would presumably, and, more importantly, properly, occasion international scandal if Germany, as part of a process of normalizing its history, put out stamps with the portraits of Hitler, Goering, or any other Nazi leaders. Indeed, one suspects that the atmosphere would be little less heated even if a German philatelic series involved great generals, and Erwin Rommell, by all accounts a military master, appeared on a German stamp.

What should one say, then, about the fact that the United States Postal Service in 1995 issued a set of stamps commemorating various figures of the Civil War (or, as was indicated in lower-point type, "The War Between the States")? At the four corners of the block are stamps commemorating four battles, Shiloh, Chancellorsville, Gettysburg, and the encounter between the Monitor and the Virginia (formerly identified as the Merrimack). The most semiotically complex of these is probably the Gettysburg stamp, which shows a Union soldier holding a gun as a club, presumably ready to come down on the Confederate soldier pointing a bayonet at his heart. More to the point, perhaps, are the stamps of individual honorees, for there on official documents of the United States of America appeared Robert E. Lee (engaging in what was apparently his third appearance on a commemorative stamp), Jefferson Davis, and "Stonewall" Jackson, among other Confederates. Especially interesting is a stamp honoring

Stand Watie, who organized a Cherokee regiment to fight on behalf of the Confederacy and was, according to the Postal Service history printed on the back of the stamp (which includes Watie's Cherokee name, De-ga-do-ga), the "last CSA General to surrender." One might interpret this simply as almost a parody of contempory political correctness, though it also points to one of the most fascinating (and, perhaps for obvious reasons) least discussed aspects of the war, which is the fact that most American Indians who participated at all did so as partisans of the slaveowning South.

As one might expect, all of these Confederate worthies were balanced in the sheet of stamps by their Union counterparts, Lincoln, Grant, Sherman, and Admiral David Farragut. (Interestingly enough, the Postal Service did not see fit to commemorate one of the two hundred thousand African Americans who Foner tells us actively fought for the Union.) The one honoree who seems without a partner is Frederick Douglass; perhaps the Postal Service just couldn't bring itself to honor George Fitzhugh, the author of the most brilliant defense of slavery, *Cannibals All*, or Edward Prigg, the Maryland slavecatcher who became the subject of an important case, *Prigg v. Pennsylvania*, in which the United States Supreme Court invalidated Pennsylvania's attempt to protect African Americans against being returned to slave states as purported "fugitive slaves."

But perhaps the perfect honoree, exquisitely capturing

the theme of unity embraced by the collection, would have been Chief Justice Roger Brooke Taney. He was at once the author of *Dred Scott*—and its holding that blacks, having "no rights which the white man was bound to respect," were ineligible to become citizens of the United States— a vigorous defender of the constitutionality of the Fugitive Slave Laws, and severe critic, during the war itself, of Lincoln's high-handedness toward those suspected of Confederate loyalties. Taney well serves to summarize many of the themes of this book, for his death in 1864 occasioned in the following year an intense debate about the propriety of following tradition and placing his bust in the chambers of the Supreme Court.[26] Charles Sumner, the great abolitionist senator from Massachusetts, who had been severely caned in 1856 by South Carolina's Preston Brooks for his views, opposed the Republican Lyman Trumbull's motion to allocate one thousand dollars to pay for a memorial bust.

> Let me tell [Senator Trumbull] that the name of Taney is to be hooted down the page of history. Judgment is beginning now; and an emancipated country will fasten upon him the stigma which he deserves. The Senator says that he for twenty-five years administered justice. He administered justice at last wickedly, and degraded the judiciary of the country, and degraded the age. . . . "Nothing but good of the dead." This is a familiar saying, which, to a cer-

tain extent, may be acknowledged. But it is entirely inapplicable when statues and busts are
proposed in honor of the dead. Then, at least,
truth must prevail. If a man has done evil during his life he must not be complimented in
marble.

Sumner was temporarily successful: Taney did not receive
his commemorative bust until after the death of his successor, Salmon P. Chase, when Congress appropriated funds
for busts of both jurists.

The central question raised by this book is whether one
ultimately sides with the intransigent, unforgiving Sumner
or the ultimately more tolerant Congress. Or, perhaps
even more accurately, when are intransigence and unfor-
givingness the appropriate responses to historical actors,
whatever the distinction of the offices they held? Senator Sumner noted that the Hall of the Doges in Venice
included "pictures of all who filled that high office in un-
broken succession, with the exception of Marino Faliero,"
who had been executed in 1355 as a traitor to the Venetian
republic. "Where his picture should have been there was a
vacant space which testified always to the justice of the republic. Let such a vacant space in our courtroom testify to
the justice of our Republic. Let it speak in warning to all
who would betray liberty. . . ." Surely the Venetians made
the correct decision, and the vacant space spoke with high
eloquence to the central values that Venice presumably

wished to inculcate in its citizens. Perhaps this is the message, for those who are aware of the Postal Service's silence, of the fact that Taney, in contrast to Jefferson Davis, has never received the degree of honor as is signified by one's presence on a commemorative stamp.

I personally have no wish whatsoever to honor, in however limited a way, Jefferson Davis, any more than Catharine MacKinnon, whom I have quoted earlier, would easily acquiesce in a decision to place Hugh Hefner on a stamp. This obviously has nothing at all to do with the significance of these men. I presume that MacKinnon would readily agree that Hefner, with his "Playboy philosophy" and magazine, is one of the true shapers of contemporary American culture, just as any objective historian would concede Davis's impact on American life in his own time. Scholars certainly should try to understand both men, and no one could cogently object to their being the subjects of probing biographies. If causal importance is enough to merit a stamp, though, then one would expect to see Al Capone or Lee Harvey Oswald gracing our nation's letters. But it is surely obvious that such causal significance is not enough to merit public homage, even the relatively limited homage that comes from being placed on a stamp. To commemorate is to take a stand, to declare the reality of heroes (or heroic events) worthy of emulation or, less frequently, that an event that occurred at a particular place was indeed so terrible that it must be remembered forever after as a cautionary note.

To be sure, the semiotician of commemorative stamps in the contemporary United States has to account for Elvis, Buddy Holly, Marilyn Monroe, and James Dean, as well as for Robert E. Lee. Perhaps the American predilection for celebrity is enough to explain all of the former. One way that the financially embattled Postal Service makes money is by putting out popular stamps that will be bought and saved, even (or especially) by noncollectors, rather than used to purchase the actual services of the agency. That being said, I remain doubtful that Hefner, easily as important (and probably as well known to most Americans) as Buddy Holly, will grace one of our stamps after his death, even if the Postal Service's marketing specialists predict that millions of would-be Playboys would buy them. Nor would I bet that General George Armstrong Custer will ever join Sitting Bull and Crazy Horse in being officially designated by the United States Postal Service as "Great Americans." As for Lee, I confess that I find him ultimately no more commendable than Custer; there is much truth in Hugh Brogan's recent denunciation of Lee as "a bloodstained traitor, one who did more damage to his country than any other in the history of the United States,"[27] though I recognize that this is a distinctly minority position within American culture (and I would criticize Lee less for being a traitor than a defender of the slavocracy in a way that, say, George Washington was not).

In any event, it seems to be as little tenable to pretend that the United States Postal Service must be neutral in regard to deciding who is fit to be commemorated as to realistically expect city councils to adopt politically neutral theories of street naming and the like. Indeed, even if offered the possibility of a scrupulously neutral state, I doubt that very many of us would accept the offer by tearing down existing monuments, prohibiting the building of new ones, and renaming all of the streets, parks, and airports after trees, oceans, and birds. To the extent that I am correct, I believe that we should have the grace to admit that our hope, when we support specific state speech in the circumstances I have been describing, is that the consciousness of the polity, especially of its future generations will be regulated in the proper direction. We might hope, for example, that the memorialization of Martin Luther King Jr. will cause current adults to refrain from casting aspersions on him. Far more important, though, is our hope that certain critical speech will not even occur to citizens of the future because it would be viewed as a blasphemy visited upon a civic icon. It should be clear that there is nothing innocent in any such hopes, that what is written in stone has no necessary permanence unless successor generations can be successfully socialized to view granite as less evanescent than a flag waving in ever-changing winds.

Notes

1 See András Gero, *Modern Hungarian Society in the Making: The Unfinished Experience,* trans. James Patterson and Eniko Koncz, chapter 11, "The Millennium Monument," pp. 203–22 (Budapest: Central European University Press, 1995). As will be true throughout this essay, I shall mainly cite scholarly sources and not offer separate citations for each quotation taken from sources that have been clearly specified in the text.

2 See Musil, "Monuments," in Burton Pike, ed., *Robert Musil: Selected Writings* (New York: Continuum, 1986), p. 320.

3 "On the Utility and Liability of History for Life," in Friedrich Nietzsche, *Unfashionable Observations,* trans. Richard T. Tray (Stanford: Stanford University Press, 1995), p. 98.

4 Alan Cowell, "Marlene's Street of Dreams? To the Barricades!" *New York Times,* 16 December 1996, p. A4. All quotations in this paragraph come from this article.

5 Kevin Sack, "Blacks Strip Slaveholders' Names Off Schools," *New York Times,* 12 November 1997, p. 1 (national edition).

6 See Michael J. Ybarra, "San Francisco Journal: Century-Old Monument Feels the Clash of History," 7 May 1996, p. A8 (national edition).

7   Kevin Sack, "Symbols of Old South Feed a New Bitterness," *New York Times,* 8 February 1997, p. 1 (national edition).

8   On "sacred space," see the important introduction by David Chidester and Edward T. Linenthal to Chidester and Linenthal, eds. *American Sacred Space* (Bloomington: University of Indiana Press, 1995), pp. 1–42.

9   Joseph Ellis, "Right Time, Wrong Place," *New York Times,* 24 March 1997, p. A21 (New England edition). Ellis objects to "the planned site for the World War II memorial, between the Washington Monument and the Lincoln Memorial. The large size of the World War II memorial—a sunken plaza flanked by two curving colonades backed by 50-foot-high walls—would mean that our most sacred space is to be occupied by a new and obtrusive tenant." The debate about the monument is well set out in Janny Scott, "Taking Its Place in U.S. History," *New York Times,* 6 March 1997, pp. D1, D6 (New England edition); Janny Scott, "Planned War Memorial Sets Off Its Own Battle in Washington," *New York Times,* 18 March 1997, pp. B1, B2 (New England edition).

10 Quoted in Michael Kammen, *Mystic Chords of Memory: The Transformation of Tradition in American Culture* (New York: Alfred A. Knopf, 1991), p. 127.

11 See Edward Linenthal, *Sacred Ground,* p. 123, n. 47 (Urbana: University of Illinois Press, 1991), citing Wallace Evans Davies, *Patriotism on Parade: The Story of Veterans and Hereditary Organizations in America, 1783–1900* (Cambridge, Mass.: Harvard University Press, 1955), p. 256. Linenthal's chapter on Gettysburg is a treasure trove of insights for anyone interested in the meaning of public monuments.

12 See Christina Cheakalos, "Monumental Debate Divides New Orleans," *Atlanta Constitution,* 15 December 1992, p. A3. The White League is briefly described by John S. Kendall in *Dic-*

tionary of American History, vol. 7 (New York: Scribner, 1976), p. 292. See generally Judith Kelleher Schafer, "The Battle of Liberty Place," in *Louisiana Cultural Vistas* 5.1 (spring 1994): 8–17. In an e-mail message, Schafer noted that of the eleven members of the Metropolitan Police who died fighting the White League, "seven were white, and none of these was native born. All were either born in Ireland or Germany, except for one Russian." Interestingly enough, the local perception in the New Orleans African American community is apparently that everyone killed by the White League in the battle was black, though this was obviously not the case.

13   Theodore Herzl, quoted in Robert Justin Goldstein, *Saving "Old Glory": The History of the American Flag Desecration Controversy* (Boulder, Colo.: Westview Press, 1995), p. ix.

14   "History and Description of the Monument in the Capitol Grounds to the Confederate Dead," in C. E. Raines, ed., *Yearbook for Texas*, vol. 11 (1903), pp. 80–82.

15   Gaines Foster, *Ghosts of the Confederacy: Defeat, the Lost Cause, and the Emergence of the New South, 1865–1913* (Baton Rouge: Louisiana State University Press, 1987), pp. 125, 194.

16   Kirk Savage, "The Politics of Memory: Black Emancipation and the Civil War Monument," in John R. Gillis, ed., *Commemorations: The Politics of National Identity* (Princeton: Princeton University Press, 1994), p. 135–36.

17   Robin W. Winks, "A Place for Liberty Monument," *New Orleans Times Picayune*, 17 August 1992, p. B7.

18   Catherine MacKinnon, *Only Words* (Cambridge: Harvard University Press, 1993), p. 31.

19   Owen M. Fiss, *State Activism and State Censorship*, Yale Law Journal 1087, 1101 (1991): 100, reprinted in Owen M. Fiss, *Liberalism Divided: Freedom of Speech and the Many Uses of State Power* (Boulder, Colo., Westview Press, 1996), p. 101. Other

quotations from Fiss come from *The Irony of Free Speech* (Cambridge: Harvard University Press, 1996).

20 Thus two early donations were statues of Alexander von Humboldt in 1869 and Giuseppe Mazzini in 1878. See Bogart, *Public Sculpture and the Civic Ideal in New York City: 1890–1930* (Chicago: University of Chicago Press, 1989), pp. 18–19. See also Edward Linenthal, *Preserving Memory: The Struggle to Create America's Holocaust Museum* (New York: Viking Press, 1995), where placement on the edge of the National Mall in Washington, and the legitimation such placement was thought to give, was an important objective of the museum's private sponsors.

21 James Forman Jr., "Driving Dixie Down: Removing the Confederate Flag from Southern State Capitols," *Yale Law Journal* 505 (1991): 101.

22 891 F.2d 1555 (1990).

23 Willie Morris, "The Ghosts of Ole Miss," in *Terrains of the Heart and Other Essays on Home* (Oxford, Miss.: Yoknapatawpha Press, 1981), p. 258.

24 Quoted in James M. Perry, "A Confederate Flag Vexes America Once Again, As Southerners Battle Each Other Over Heritage," *Wall Street Journal*, 4 February 1997, p. A20.

25 See Patricia Nelson Limerick, "The Battlefield of History," *New York Times*, 28 August 1997, p. A37.

26 The debate can be found in Paul Finkelman, ed., *Dred Scott v. Sandford: A Brief History with Documents* (Boston: Bedford Books, 1997), p. 220–26.

27 See Brogan's review of Ernest B. Furgurson, *Ashes of Glory: Richmond at War, New York Times Book Review,* 29 September 1996, p. 24. Part of the power of Brogan's comment undoubtedly comes from the fact that it so dramatically counters the veneration of Lee that has become part of official American culture.

Sanford Levinson is Professor of Law at the University
of Texas at Austin. He has authored and edited a number
of books including *Constitutional Faith* and *Interpreting Law
and Literature* (with Steven Mailloux).

Library of Congress Cataloging-in-Publication Data
Levinson, Sanford.
Written in stone: public monuments in changing societies /
Sanford Levinson.
p.   cm. — (Public planet books)
ISBN 0-8223-2204-8 (alk. paper).
ISBN 0-8223-2220-x (pbk. : alk. paper)
1. Monuments—Political aspects—United States.   2. Flags—
Political aspects—United States.   3. Multiculturalism—United
States.   4. Political culture—United States—History—20th century.
I. Title.   II. Series.
E159.L485   1998   306.2—dc21   97-49361 CIP